GHOSTS AND CURSES IN THE BIBLE

DYLAN CLEARFIELD

Copyright © 2017 Prism Thomas

Published by the G. Stempien Publishing Company
Blessed Isle, Wales, UK

CONTENTS

INTRODUCTION

The Bible is filled with ghosts and ghostly encounters. Both the Old Testament and the New Testament as well as many books of the Apocrypha, particularly the Books of Maccabees and the works of Josephus. This shouldn't be surprising since the Bible and its related literature is closely linked with the supernatural. This only makes sense when taking into account that God Himself is believed to be either the author of the Bible or at the very least its direct inspiration.

Assuming that there are instances in the Bible where ghosts are described and alluded to, what does this imply concerning the reality of ghosts? It seems clear that this would confer great validity to the existence of ghosts. If God Himself speaks of ghosts as entities that exist, they MUST exist!

Bringing to light stories about ghosts within the Bible and related writings is what this book is about. Firstly, it is important to note at the outset what is meant by the term ghost. For our purposes, a ghost is a disembodied spirit of a formerly living creature. This includes both Jesus and his mother, Mary.

As important as the definition of a ghost, is the determination of what a ghost is not. Angels and demons are not ghosts. Neither angels nor demons have been natural living creatures of the earth – they are supernatural by nature, spirit in form. They cannot be ghosts.

A critical point to make here is that according to the Bible God created a class of beings known as angels. Angels are special spiritual beings without body or substance. Angels **ARE NOT** what people become after they die. This is a gross misconception of current culture. A species of angels was created at **one time only** by God. Death does not create any more of them.

Also ruled out from the class of beings known as ghosts are visions. Forms seen by saints, mystics or even ordinary people in ecstatic states do not qualify as ghosts – they are visions. This isn't to say that saints, mystics and prophets have never seen ghosts, just that visions and ghosts are not the same thing.

What is meant by the term vision? A vision is an experience – not necessarily visual – had by an individual to which no one else is a witness. It's more of an internal event of some profound significance to that person alone.

There are occurrences – like at Fatima – where more than one person witnesses a visionary event, but this is clearly of a religious nature, not a ghost sighting. Also, there have been occasions of mass hallucinations or even mass confusion and these events would not be considered ghost sightings either. Not any more than a UFO sighting.

This is not to rule out sightings of the Virgin Mary and Jesus from the list of ghost sightings. A number of these are included in the book. Why couldn't the ghost of Jesus have been seen? He'd once been a living being on the planet and had died. As such, Jesus could have and did produce ghostly apparitions.

Ghostly sightings of Mary pose a special problem. Among some belief systems – particularly Roman Catholic – Mary never died but was assumed into heaven. Can a person who'd never died have a ghost? Yes. It is well known and verified that a human being while still alive can project a ghostly form. This is not astral projection or bi-location, but the appearance of the actual ghost of a living being. It's a very fine distinction, but an important one.

These are the basic ground rules for this book. Others will be added later as needed but the ones just set out are most important.

SAUL'S SUPERNATURAL ENCOUNTERS

Saul's encounter with the ghost of Samuel is one of the oldest ghost stories on record. It took place in 1013 B.C. and is documented in the Books of Samuel, Chronicles, and Kings. It's important to examine all the accounts of Saul's raising of the ghost of Samuel because some accounts add more and different details than others. They aren't simply carbon copies of the same story.

Saul was a person entangled in the occult and who had more than one supernatural encounter. In addition to his meeting with Samuel's ghost, Saul also was once plagued by an evil spirit.

Many authorities claim that this evil spirit wasn't a true entity but that it was a personification of a mental illness. However, Scripture specifically states that it was an evil spirit that beset Saul: 1 SAMUEL 16: 14. "Now the spirit of the Lord departed from Saul, and an evil spirit from the Lord tormented him."

It's difficult to be clearer than that. Scripture doesn't say that Saul was suffering from a mental illness or that he heard strange voices in his head.   Scripture says directly that an EVIL SPIRIT from the Lord tormented him.

This is important because when deciphering stories from Scripture it is crucial to know if what is being described is meant to be literal or allegorical.   Can a person ever know for sure?   Yes.   A close reading of Scripture reveals that when something is meant to be allegorical, qualifying words are used.   Words such as: like, almost, as if.   When something is to be understood in a literal sense there is a lack of qualifying words.

An evil spirit from the Lord tormented Saul.   That is a literal statement.   A qualifying statement would be: It was as if an evil spirit tormented Saul.   This is not a literal statement.   Those two statements are very different.

Another proof that it was literally an evil spirit tormenting Saul is given by the reaction of his servants. "Behold," one of them remarks, "now an evil spirit from the Lord is tormenting you."

Saul's servants recognized the presence of a demon.   If the evil spirit was merely the product of Saul's hallucinating then his delusion was potent enough to affect his servants as well.   Does this seem more likely than Saul literally being beset by an evil spirit?

This is important because revisionists of God's words have

attempted to describe practically every miraculous event in the Bible as nothing more than an allegory. While many people have chosen to discredit miracles, I am not one of them. And when a person reads the accounts in the Bible at face value he will find that there is a great deal of supernatural activity taking place.

Saul had many encounters with the supernatural. He consulted soothsayers more than once and got in trouble for it more than once.

On the night prior to the raising of Samuel's spirit, Saul found himself greatly troubled over the impending battle with the Philistines. He was anxious to know the outcome and he sought advice from the Lord but received no response. Saul then questioned his priests and prophets for any information they might have on the outcome of the battle but they wouldn't help him either.

Saul was clearly distraught. He was no longer on good terms with the Lord and he faced an impending military battle whose outcome was in serious doubt. His next step was to try to divine the future himself. Using a divination method known as the urin and thummin – casting of lots with sacred objects – he attempted to get insight into the future. This also failed.

Saul was desperate, and he once again turned to his servants for advice. Hadn't they already helped him ward off an evil spirit?

This time they directed him to a witch who practiced an ancient Canaanite version of divination by necromancy – raising the spirits of the dead to question them about the future. She was the infamous witch of Endor and Saul's apparent last choice.

This presented a major problem for Saul because Endor was situated near Mount Gilboa which was well behind enemy lines. This entire area was a historically significant site to the Israelites. Hundreds of years previously this important locus of the caravan routes was controlled by the Canaanites. The Canaanites kept everyone in this region under subjugation, including the Israelites. At that time, another momentous battle was fought here as the oppressed peoples joined together in their struggle for independence from the Canaanites.

There is also a very beautiful story associated with this part of the country. According to Israelite legend, this was the site of a sacred tree under which the Israelite prophetess Deborah often sat while in communication with her Lord. From beneath the cover of the blessed boughs Deborah would transmit the word of God to His chosen people.

One of these messages from Deborah concerned an upcoming battle with the Canaanites. Deborah was supplied with crucial military instructions from the Lord which she was told to report to the generals of the allied armies. First, she was to advise them to attack the Canaanites on the morrow. Then she was to instruct the allied armies to march their warriors to Mount Tabor and there to organize and prepare for battle.

This seemed contrary to sound military strategy. The Israelites had a lightly armed force and waging a direct assault against a much more heavily armed Canaanite army seemed doomed to disaster.

Nonetheless, those were the orders from the Lord and the Israelites and their allies obeyed them, perhaps thinking that the Lord was preparing them for a sacrificial slaughter. God was actually setting the stage for a stunning Israelite victory.

On the day of the battle there was a mighty deluge, turning the battlefield into a quagmire. The ponderous chariots and war machines of the Canaanites were hopelessly bogged down in the mud and the lightly armed Israelites easily outfought them. The victory of the Israelites was overwhelming, resulting in the death of the hated Canaanite Prince Sisera who was ignominiously killed when struck in the head with a mallet by a Kentite woman while he was drinking from a bowl of milk.

Now, many decades later, the Israelites were on the eve of another battle in the same location. Anxious about the outcome, Saul travelled seven miles beyond enemy lines in heavy disguise to seek aid from the Witch of Endor.

The Witch of Endor lived in a spooky grotto inside of Mount Gilboa and performed many of her rituals before the waters of the natural fountain that echoed through the cavernous realm. Saul entered the grotto alone and approached the witch. He told her that he wanted to speak to the spirit of the recently departed King of the Israelites, Samuel. What follows is a description of Saul's meeting with the Witch of Endor as it is recorded in 1 Samuel 28:11-19.

[11] Then the woman said, "Who shall I bring up for you?" He said, "Bring up Samuel for me." [12] When the woman saw Saul, she cried out with a loud voice; and the woman said to Saul, "Why have you deceived me? You are Saul."

[13]The king said to her, "Have no fear; what do you see?" And the woman said to Saul, I see a god coming up out of the earth." [14]He said to her, "What is his appearance?" and she said, "An old man is coming up; and he is wrapped in a robe." And Saul knew that it was Samuel, and he bowed his face to the ground and did

obeisance.""

At this point, a comment is in order. Many people claim that Saul never really saw the ghost of Samuel but that it was the Witch of Endor who told him who the spirit was and convinced Saul that it was Samuel that had risen. Note the last line of verse 14: And Saul knew that it was Samuel, and he bowed his face to the ground and did obeisance. Also note that when asked what she saw in regards to the spirit, that the witch at no time described the spirit specifically as Samuel. She described the ghost as: 1)a god, and 2)an old man.

With those points made, continue with the biblical account from verse 15.

[15]Then Samuel said to Saul, "Why have you disturbed me by bringing me up?" Saul answered, "I am in great distress; for the Philistines are warring against me, and God has turned away from me and answers me no more, either by prophets or dreams; therefore I have summoned you to tell me what I shall do."

[16]And Samuel said, "Why then do you ask me, since the Lord has

turned from you and become your enemy? [17]The Lord has done to you as He spoke by me; for the Lord has torn the kingdom out of your hands and given it to your neighbor, David. [18]Because you did not obey the voice of the Lord, and did not carry out His fierce wrath against Amalek, therefore the Lord has done this thing to you this day. [19]Moreover, the Lord will give Israel also with you into the hands of the Philistines; and tomorrow you and your sons shall be with me; the Lord will give the army of Israel also into the hands of the Philistines."

Thus spoke the ghost of Samuel, and everything that was predicted came to pass. On the next day the army of Israel under the leadership of Saul met the Philistines and the Israelites were crushed. Saul and his able-bodied sons were killed. It is believed that Saul either fell on his own sword or that he was killed by an Amalekite camp follower upon Saul's request.

In any event, both Saul and his sons were later impaled over the gates of Beth-Shean. And thus was the prophecy of the ghost of Samuel fulfilled. It would seem clear that by anyone's definition this was a ghost story. And there are many more stories in the Bible that it would be difficult to describe as anything but a ghost story.

PHANTOM HANDWRITING

Does the story about the handwriting on the wall classify as a ghost story? Most people who read this passage from the Bible don't recognize it as a ghostly event. They simply see it as an act of God. The true secret lies in uncovering whose hand is doing the writing. The Bible does not say that the handwriting was done by the hand of God, only that the message was inspired by God. Who performed the actual writing? Biblical detective work will be required to answer this question.

The story of the handwriting on the wall takes place during a dramatic period in history. At the centre of the story is the famed prophet Daniel who is also responsible for many apocalyptic revelations.

It was 539 B.C. and the Chaldean Empire was under a blistering assault from the Persian army under the ultimate control of the famous King Cyrus. Babylon was the capital of Chaldea and was supposedly under the protection of crown prince Belshazzar. Supposedly so because Belshazzar was more interested in carousing than in protecting the nation's capital.

In some accounts Belshazzar is identified as the son of the famous king Nebuchadnezzar II and in some accounts Belshazzar is referred to as the king of Chaldea. Both descriptions of him are erroneous. The actual king was Nabonidus – not Nebuchadnezzar II – and, as already noted, Belshazzar was a prince not a king. Belshazzar was the son of Nabonidus and Nebuchadnezzar II was in reality an ally-by-marriage rather than a close blood relation to either of them.

At the time that the story takes place the city of Babylon is under attack by one of King Cyrus's most devoted generals, a man named Gobryas. Gobryas was so determined to take this city that he diverted the course of the great Euphrates River in order to take Babylon by surprise.

While the king of Chaldea – Nabonidus – was battling a Persian onslaught at Borsippa, Gobryas marched unopposed toward the gates of Babylon. Where was Belshazzar? Why wasn't he defending the city's gates? He was busy throwing a huge feast at his palace.

Belshazzar was overseeing a great orgiastic affair. This was indicated by the presence of women whose only purpose for attending feasts during this time period in the ancient East was to provide sexual entertainment.

This was such a large affair that additional plates and goblets had to be located to accommodate all the guests. The plates and goblets brought out weren't just any plates and goblets but they were taken from the store of sacred vessels that had been stolen from the temple in Jerusalem when it was ransacked by the Chaldeans in 580 B.C.. Now they were being used for carousing during an orgy.

It was probably this sacrilegious act that caused the direful message of wrath to suddenly be written on the banquet wall for all to see and fear. Screams replaced the laughter and blissful moaning as phantom fingers appeared from nowhere and wrote on the plaster wall under the full light of a well-placed lamp stand.

Belshazzar was struck with terror, crying out in alarm, "In great earnest!" In his culture, these words had the same meaning as, "God help us!" would have in American culture. The Bible describes the crown prince as changing color and having his limbs give way. In other words – he nearly fainted.

It is highly significant that the spectral handwriting appeared at a place on the wall which was usually reserved for national memorials. It certainly seemed to be designed to desecrate their revered wall to a similar degree in which the people of Israel's sacred vessels had been desecrated.

The message was written in Aramaic – a major language of the period – and, while the words were in themselves understandable, the context in which they appeared was not. This was the message: MENE, MENE, TEKEL, PERES. The words represented units of measure and weight. It would be like writing: a bag of quarters, an ounce, and a half gallon. What does that mean!

The word mene meant fifty sheckles and was also the equivalent of two pounds by weight. Tekel was equivalent to a single Hebrew sheckle and as such would weigh about an ounce.

It must have meant something of great importance since it was written by a terrifying spectral hand. But no one knew what it was supposed to mean. Thus Belshazzar summoned his best soothsayers, astrologers and wizards to give him an answer. But they couldn't. None of them could decipher the message. Maybe they couldn't do so because, as it was stated so well in 1 Corinthians 1:21 "they know not God."

At this point, Belshazzar's mother – Queen Nitocris – suggested that one of the captives from Judah be summoned to help. Daniel was known to possess prophetic powers, and he was brought to the banquet hall.

Daniel studied the writing on the wall, took a moment for contemplation, and then offered his divinely inspired interpretation as in Daniel 5:22-28.

[22]And you his son, Belshazzar, have not humbled your heart, though you knew all this, [23]but you have lifted up yourself against the Lord of

heaven; and the vessels of his house have been brought in before you, and you and your lords, your wives, and your concubines have drunk wine from them; and you have praised the gods of silver and gold, of bronze, iron, wood and stone, which do not see or hear or know, but the God in whose hand is your breath, and whose are all your ways, you have not honored.

[24]"Then from His presence the hand was sent, and this writing was described. [25]And this is the writing that was inscribed: MENE, MENE, TEKEL, and, PARSIN. (Note – the word PARSIN is not a typo. Daniel used this word instead of Peres but never explains why.)

[26]This is the interpretation of the matter: MENE, God has numbered the days of your kingdom and brought it to an end; [27]TEKEL, you have been weighed in the balances and found wanting; [28]PERES, your kingdom is divided and given to the Medes and Persians."

Belshazzar was alarmed by the reading of the message on the wall. To reward Daniel, he immediately had him clothed in royal robes of purple and placed the golden chain of office around his neck. Or was this to make Daniel the obvious target of the enemy invaders when they stormed into the city so that they would execute him instead of Belshazzar?

If that was Belshazzar's plan it didn't work. Hours later Gobryas led his army into Babylon and the first person executed was Belshazzar. Daniel was spared and taken into custody.

Such were the historical events on the night of the handwriting on the wall. But whose spectral hand was it that wrote the message of doom on the wall? Most people assume it was the hand of God, but Daniel never identified the hand as belonging to God. In fact, he only said that it was sent by God: "Then from His presence the hand was sent…" The wording here is very important: "…the hand was sent…" If it had been God's hand, the wording would have been much different.

Whose hand was it! It isn't likely that the hand belonged to an angel. Throughout the Bible whenever angels are used as God's messengers they are identified as angels.

Are there any clues as to the hand's identity? One clue would be the content of the message itself. It was prophetic – a warning to Belshazzar. Perhaps God had sent a prophet of old to deliver the written prophecy. Which prophet of old? There's quite a long list of them from which to select.

But among all of the prophets there is one who is credited with having written a posthumous letter of prophecy. Elijah! Earlier, a letter written by Elijah had been delivered after his death to one of the Israelite leaders prophesying doom. Was it the spirit of Elijah who wrote the handwriting on the wall?

If only a comparison could be made between Elijah's posthumous letter and the handwriting on the wall. Would they match?

One thing is certain: a spectral hand appeared in Babylon on the night in question and it did write a prophetic message on the wall. There are dozens of witnesses to this and it is documented in the Bible.

It would be classified as a form of spirit writing. Spirit writing in general is a relatively common way to communicate with the other side. However, the actual act of writing is usually performed by a living being through the inspiration of a spirit. The hand of the medium is controlled by the spirit. Very rarely does a spirit hand materialize to do the writing.

There are two important occasions in which a hand of the spirit materialized. They are described in the book, *The Debatable Land* Between *this World and the Next* by the well-known 19th century theologian and author, Robert Dale Owen. This book was published in 1871 by G. W. Carlton & Company of London, England.

The first séance was one which Mr. Owen personally attended and was conducted by Kate Fox one of the famous Fox sisters who was credited with reviving modern spiritualism in 1848. It was a private sitting with only the two in attendance and it occurred on August 8, 1861 at Mrs. Fox's home on West 46th Street in New York City.

To reduce the possibility of deception Mr. Owen locked the doors and windows to the room which was further closed off with a wax seal that was marked with an impression from his signet ring. After doing this, he placed strips of paper and a pencil on the table for the use of any spirit which chose to write a message.

The séance began as normal. Soon thereafter a spectral hand materialized, took up the pencil, and began to write on the available paper. The spirit wrote the following message in a steady, natural motion:

The night is not favourable for appearing. I will soon
Overcome difficulties. You shall see, believe me.

The spectral hand signed her name and it proved to be that of an old acquaintance of Mr. Owens'.

Another instance of a ghostly hand being observed while writing took place on August 18, 1861 where the same Kate Fox held a sitting for a

Mr. Livermore. This also was documented in Mr. Owens' book that was previously mentioned. Mister Livermore brought with him two large blank cards which he'd specially marked to guard against trickery. These were for the spirits to write on.

After the room was prepared for the séance Mr. Livermore placed the cards on the table along with a special pencil. He then clasped the medium's hands in his to prevent fraud.

The séance began. A spectral hand appeared, picked up the pencil and primed it over the cards. It was a hand like any other hand but was disembodied. For nearly an hour the hand wrote its message on the cards before vanishing.

Thus, the handwriting on the wall in the biblical account was not in itself unique or without similar occurrences with which it could be compared.

Spectral hands in one form or another have made appearances in various ways, aside from writing messages. One of the more popular methods of making their presence known is by leaving scorch mark impressions. In many of these instances the background of the event is religious in nature. Another connection with the handwriting on the wall?

Many years ago a member of a Czechoslovakian family was visited by a hand from Purgatory. The spirit of a man who was suffering in Purgatory was allowed to visit the earth to give a message to a surviving son. The son had recently fulfilled a vow to his deceased father – the spirit in question - that he would make a pilgrimage to a holy shrine. The spirit of his father appeared to him while he was at prayer one morning and acknowledged the fulfilment of the vow. As proof of his presence, the spirit had scorched a handprint into one of the pages on the inside of the recipient's prayer book. The spirit informed the son where to look and when he looked through his prayer book he located the handprint which matched that of his father's.

A similar story comes from Saar, Germany. Mass was being said for a deceased priest when handprints were supernaturally scorched into the liturgical missal from which the presiding clergyman was reading. The handprints were scorched into selected sites throughout the missal, marking passages that had been of particular importance to the deceased priest.

Another account comes from Krakow, Poland where a property dispute in 1637 was waged between a widow and a wealthy landowner. The landowner won his case by bribing the court. Enraged at the judge, the widow nodded toward a cross of Jesus on the wall in the courtroom and chastised, "If Satan himself were judge, he'd give a fairer judgement."

Satan must have been listening. A demonic handprint was deeply scorched into the tabletop over which the widow was braced when she made her accusation. This sign of Satan's visit was discovered the next day by the clerk of the court and caused a great uproar.

Yet another account comes from the 17th century and involves a hermit who had inexplicably developed a close friendship with the dean of Thaur University, Georg Meringer. It's inexplicable because hermits are not known for having close friends. At any rate – the two close friends made a pact the type that were common down through the centuries: whoever died first would in some way give a sign to the other, verifying the existence of the afterlife.   The hermit was the first to pass on.

One night in October of 1659 the ghost of the hermit appeared to Father Meringer as he peacefully tended a decorative box of flowers. The ghost was there not only to announce the existence of an afterlife but he was there to reprimand the good father for having failed to recite two masses for the dead which had already been paid for.

As proof of his visit, the hermit burned his handprint into the bottom of the box of flowers.

What to make of all these handprints being scorched into various mediums throughout the centuries? While not a common everyday occurrence it's not an event that is exceptionally out of the ordinary either.

What does a handprint represent? Maybe the soul. A hand is a significant feature of a human being and to touch a person's hand might be a way to touch that person's soul as well.

Whose soul was responsible for the famous handwriting on the wall? A prime candidate is Elijah for the reasons given previously.

APPARITIONS OF JESUS

Can Jesus Christ have a ghost? Jesus was once a living being on the earth and he had a human form. This is basically the only requirement for a person to be able to produce a ghost.

But Jesus! A ghost? Let's look at the facts. For forty days after His death and resurrection there were many sightings of Jesus. If this wasn't a ghost, how else would the sightings of him be described?

Jesus had not yet ascended into heaven. That's why these forty days were so important. He was still subject to the natural laws that all human beings are subject to. Most people seem to miss this point. But it's the very point which makes His resurrection so astonishing. Jesus was a man who literally came back from the dead. How many other people have done this by their own power?

But was it His ghost that people saw? Let's examine the facts of the matter.

The first apparition of Jesus took place on that first Easter morning (John 20: 1,2). Mary Magdalene was the first of the followers of Jesus to arrive at his tomb in order to anoint His body for burial. She found the tomb empty. Her first response was to rush to Peter and John and tell them that someone had taken the Lord's body. The three hurried back to the tomb and found the body gone and only the burial linens still there. Peter and John departed in bewilderment. Mary remained outside the tomb, weeping.

Peeking inside the tomb once more, Mary beheld two angels. The following is what occurred next (John 20: 13-18).

[13]They said to her, "Woman, why are you weeping?" She said to them, "Because they have taken away the Lord, and I do not know where they have laid him." [14]Saying this, she turned around and saw Jesus standing, but did not know that it was Jesus. [15]Jesus said to her, "Woman, why are you weeping? Whom do you seek?" Supposing him to be the gardener, she said to him, "Sir, if you have carried him away, tell me where you have laid him, and I will take him away."

[16]Jesus said to her,"Mary." She turned and said to him in Hebrew, "Rabboni!" (which means teacher). [17]Jesus said to her, "Do not hold me, for I have yet to ascend to the Father; but go to my brethren and say to them, I am ascending to my Father and your Father, to my God and your God." [18]Mary Magdalene went and said to the disciples, "I have seen the

Lord;" and she told them that he had said these things to her.

The Jesus that Mary Magdalene saw was certainly in a different form than the Jesus she had seen in life. It is very important to note that at first sight she did not even recognize Him. He surely had "supernatural" abilities at this time, having appeared as if from nowhere and then vanishing in the same manner. This is definitely ghostly behavior.

The second encounter with Jesus after the resurrection took place a short time later to a number of women who'd belonged to the group who'd stood at the bottom of the Cross of Jesus. Included in this gathering was; Mary, the mother of James, Joanna, the wife of Chuza – Herod's steward – and Salome. Like Mary Magdalene they were also heading toward the sepulchre to anoint the body of Jesus for burial. When they reached the tomb they found two angels who instructed them to relay the news of the resurrection of Jesus to the disciples. While they hurried from the tomb to give the good news to the disciples they met the spirit of Jesus (Matthew 28: 9,10).

[9]And behold, Jesus met them and said, "Hail!" and they came up and took hold of his feet and worshiped him. [10]Then Jesus said to them, "Do

not be afraid; go and tell my brethren to go to Galilee, and there they will see me."

The following account of a visitation by the spirit of Jesus is one of the most ghost-like of encounters. It has all the elements of a typical apparition and took place shortly after His resurrection. It is of such importance to this compilation of sightings that it will be related at length exactly as it is described in the Bible (Luke 24: 13-31).

[13]That very day two of them were going to the village named Emmaus about seven miles from Jerusalem, [14]and talking with each other about all these things that had happened.

[15]While they were talking and discussing together, Jesus himself drew near and went with them. [16]But their eyes were kept from recognizing him. [17]And he said to them, "What is this conversation which you are holding with each other as you walk?" And they stood still, looking sad. [18]Then one of them, named Cleopas, answered him, "Are you the only visitor to Jerusalem who does not know the things that have happened here in these days?"

[19]And he said to them, "What things?" And they said to him, "Concerning Jesus of Nazareth, who was a prophet mighty in deed and word before God and all the people, [20]and how our chief priests and rulers delivered him up to be condemned to death, and crucified him. [21]But we had hoped that he was the one to redeem Israel. Yes, and besides all this, it is the third day since this happened.

[22]Moreover,some women of our company amazed us. They were at the tomb early in the morning [23]and did not find his body; and they came back saying that they had even seen a vision of angels, who said that he wasalive. [24]Some of them who were with us went to the tomb, and found it just as the women had said; but they did not see him." [25] And he said to them, "Oh

foolish men, and slow of heart to believe all that prophets had spoken! [26]Was it not necessary that the Christ should suffer these things and enter his glory?" [27]And beginning with Moses and all the prophets, he interpreted to them in all the scriptures the things concerning himself.

[28]So they drew near to the village to which they were going. He

appeared to be going further, [29]but they constrained him, saying, "Stay with us for it is toward evening and the day is far spent." So he went in to stay with them. [30]When he was at table with them, he took the bread and blessed, and broke it, and gave it to them. [31]And their eyes were opened and they recognized him; and he vanished out of their sight.

And he vanished out of their sight! This sounds like ghostly activity. In fact, it would be hard to view this as anything other than a ghostly encounter with Christ. He appears out of nowhere, visits for a time, then disappears into nowhere.

Once again, Jesus is not immediately recognized by the people he's visiting. They have no idea who he is. These are strangers, however, who may never have seen him. But they knew OF him. And once Jesus broke and blessed the bread at the dinner table with them they recognized who He was. Then He vanished

Jesus' next appearance was at meal time again. This time it was breakfast. Several of the apostles had been fishing in the Sea of Tiberius and were about to eat some of their catch. Once again, the witnesses to the apparition at first did not recognise Jesus – his own former apostles. This is how it was described in John 21: 2-12.

[2]Simon Peter, Thomas called the twin, Nathanael of Cana in Galilee, the sons of Zebedee, and two other of his disciples were together. [3]Simon Peter said to them, "I am going fishing." They said to him, "We will go with you." They went out and got into the boat; but that night they caught nothing. [4]Just as day was breaking, Jesus stood on the beach; yet the disciples did not know it was Jesus. [5]Jesus said to them, "Children, have you any fish?" They answered him, "No." [6]He said to them, "Cast the net on the right side of the boat, and you will find some." So they cast it, and now they were not able to haul it in, for the quantity of fish. [7]The disciple whom Jesus loved said to Peter, "It is the Lord!" When Simon Peter heard that it was the Lord, he put on his clothes, for he was stripped for work, and sprang into the sea. [8]But the other disciples came in the boat, dragging the net full of fish, for they were not far from the land, but about a hundred yards off.

[9]When they got out on land, they saw a charcoal fire there, with fish lying on it, and bread. [10]Jesus said to them, "Bring some of the fish that you have just caught." [11]So Simon Peter went aboard and hauled the net ashore, full of large fish, a hundred and fifty of them; and all though there

were too many of them the net was not torn.   [12]Jesus said to them, "Come and have breakfast.   Now none of the disciples dared to ask him, "Who are you?"

Why doesn't anyone seem to recognize Jesus after His death and resurrection? Had he changed that much? Could it be a physical trait common to ghostly forms?

Jesus acts like many ghosts act after having met a sudden, tragic end to life. He acted if nothing had changed; as if everything were normal. This is a very common ghostly attribute. Often, the spirit of the deceased is not aware that death has occurred and attempts to resume life as normal.

Is this what the ghost of Jesus is doing? It certainly seems something similar to this.

Another important apparition of Jesus is His famous roadside appearance to Saul(Paul) as he was on his way to Damascus. This took place well after the resurrection and Christ's ascension.

Paul had studied under Rabbi Gamaliel and shared the teacher's vehement hatred of the sect of Jewish-Christians which had arisen after Jesus' resurrection. It is believed that Paul had even taken an active part in the stoning of Saint Stephen.

Saul went to the high priests of Jerusalem and sought and received permission to make a trip to Damascus for the purpose of gathering up and bringing back in chains as many Christians as he could. The fateful trip was going to be interrupted (Acts 9: 3-7).

[3]Now as he journeyed he approached Damascus, and suddenly a light from heaven flashed around him. [4]And he fell to the ground and heard a voice saying to him, "Saul, Saul why do you persecute me?" [5]And he said, "Who are you, Lord?" And he said, "I am Jesus, whom you are persecuting; [6]but rise and enter the city, and you will be told what to do." [7]The men who were travelling with him stood speechless, hearing the voice but seeing no one.

Importantly, the people travelling with Paul also heard the voice of Jesus. Thus, this was not simply an ecstatic vision had by Paul alone but it was a true supernatural event experienced by more than one person.

Even though Jesus was not seen on this occasion, he was heard. Hearing ghostly voices qualifies as a supernatural encounter as well.

It's important again to note the difference between a vision and a ghostly sighting and how in these instances Jesus is more ghostlike than vision like. Had these been visions Jesus would have maintained a type of "spectral distance" rather than becoming involved in a one-on-one situation with those he was visiting.

The ghost of Jesus made many appearances around Jerusalem after his crucifixion.   Then he ascended to heaven.

JESUS LOOK-ALIKES

Has the apparition of Jesus appeared in modern times? There have been many claims of such sightings but they are very different from the initial ones shortly after His crucifixion and may not be what they seem.

A former pastor of the Pentecostal Holiness Church in Oakland, California claimed a close encounter with Jesus in April of 1954. During a late Sunday night service while the pastor preached to a congregation of about fifty people an eerie, shadowy form appeared on the glass door which led into the church from outside.

The door opened and a tall, bearded man who fit the description of Jesus Christ entered. He strolled down the central aisle, smiling and blessing the people he passed, and then joined the minister on the speaker's platform. The Jesus look-alike placed a hand on the pastor's shoulder, apparently causing the preacher to faint. The figure knelt beside him, spoke to him in a foreign language which the minister somehow understood, then vanished.

Five years later, a similar event occurred in the same church. On a day in May in 1959 one of the female members of the church took the pulpit to talk about the just described event. She disappeared and was replaced by the form of Jesus. He revealed his palms to the crowd of almost two hundred stunned people, displaying the signs of His crucifixion. Someone in the crowd had a movie camera and caught it all on film. Jesus – or his counterpart - visited for only a short time before disappearing and being replaced by the female speaker who had no recollection of where she had gone.

The film of the event was viewed by many but has mysteriously disappeared. Do not most such films seem to mysteriously disappear?

Do the two preceding occurrences qualify as apparitions of Jesus? They seem very suspicious. Why? They have the appearances of well-planned hoaxes, meaning that the events occurred as if in a staged manner.

In regard to the second event: how did the person who played the part of Jesus vanish? And where did the female church member go when Jesus appeared in her stead? And what about the film?

Magicians have many ways to make a person vanish, as well as replace one object on a stage with another object. Maybe it was all a magician's trick.

Isn't the proof on the film?   Not any more – if it ever was.   Even the mysterious disappearance of the film is very hoax-like.   It's also very reminiscent of all the UFO films and photographs that had suddenly vanished.

But the most difficult aspect to reconcile with true ghostly activity between these two Jesus sightings and the biblical ones is the way that the supposed Jesus acted.   Compare how He interacted with the people in the church with the way He interacted with those he encountered shortly after His crucifixion.

The person who entered the church in the guise of Jesus lacked the openness and naturalism of the Jesus who appeared to the disciples.   It was as if he were performing on cue and avoiding any attempt at close contact with anyone except those who were part of the script in fear that his true identity would be revealed.

It's highly doubtful that the person who made the two appearances at the Pentecostal Holiness Church were apparitions of the real Jesus.

There is another apparition of Jesus of note which occurred in modern day China.   What makes it particularly interesting is that it is an apparent case of time shifting where an event of the past is replayed before a contemporary audience.

It took place before a large, non-Christian group of would-be converts to whom the gospel was being preached. Fortunately, the event was witnessed by an assistant to a U.S. Congressman who was on a fact finding mission to China at the time. Otherwise the occurrence would probably never have been exposed to the world.

While the gospel was being preached, a scene from the past was projected onto the air. The passion of Jesus was displayed before the onlookers as if by miraculous design. This would certainly qualify as a ghostly apparition since in form it was exactly like more common hauntings in which images of the past are depicted on the air.

It seems that Jesus does still make appearances in the world but at only select locations and extremely rarely. Since ascending into heaven, His appearances also are of a different nature, more like images replayed in the ether rather than as an interactive spirit. Jesus is still with us in many ways.

JESUS HAS HIS OWN GHOSTLY ENCOUNTER

What if Jesus saw a ghost? What if he saw more than one ghost? He did. One does not usually associate the Transfiguration of Christ with a ghostly sighting, but if taken at face value, that is exactly what it was. And who could possibly be a more credible witness than Jesus Christ?

About a week before the Transfiguration Jesus had a series of intense conversations with his closest disciples which in a sense sets the stage for the great supernatural event to come (Luke 9: 18-23).

[18]Now it happened as he was praying alone the disciples were with him; and he asked them, "Who do the people say that I m?" [19]And they answered, "John the Baptist; but others say, Elijah; and others, that one of the old prophets has risen." [20]And he said to them, "But who do you say that I am?" And Peter answered, "The Christ of God." [21]But he charged and commanded them to tell this to no one, [22]saying, "The Son of man must suffer many things, and be rejected by the elders and the chief priests and scribes, and be killed, and on thethird day be raised.

[23]And he said to all, "If any man would come after me, let him deny himself and take up his cross dailyand follow me..."

About eight days after this powerful talk, Jesus took Peter, James and John with Him to pray on Mount Hermon 9000 feet above sea level. Tradition names the mountain as Mount Tabor but since Mount Hermon is only twelve miles northeast of Caesarea Phillipi where Jesus and the disciples had been staying prior to the Transfiguration the actual location of the event would most likely have been Mount Hermon.

The transfiguration is one of the most profound occurrences in the life of Jesus during which the divine light of God blazed within Him to reveal His true nature as the Son of God. This is where He and his apostles encountered a pair of biblical ghosts (Luke 9: 28-36).

[28]Now about eight days after these sayings he took with him Peter and John and James, and went up on the mountain to pray. [29]And as he was praying, the appearance of his countenance was altered, and his raiment became dazzling white. [30]And behold, two men talked with him, Moses and Elijah, [31]who appeared in glory and spoke of his departure, which he

was to accomplish at Jerusalem. [32]Now Peter and those who were with him were heavy with sleep but kept awake, and they saw his glory and the two men who stood with him. [33]And as the men were parting from him, Peter said to Jesus, "Master, it is well that we are here; let us make three booths, one for you and one for Moses and one for Elijah" not knowing what he had said. [34]As he said this, a cloud came and overshadowed them; and they were afraid as they entered the cloud. [35]and a voice came out of the cloud, saying, "This is my Son, My chosen; Listen to Him!" [36]And when the voice had spoken, Jesus was found alone. And they kept silence and told no one in those days anything of what they had seen.

What Jesus and the three disciples saw were certainly the ghosts of Moses and Elijah. How else could someone describe what they had seen? Both Moses and Elijah were deceased and it was their spirits to whom Jesus had spoken on the mountain top.

While it can be argued that Elijah had never "officially" died – having been swept up into heaven in a fiery chariot on a whirlwind – there could be no doubt that Moses had been long dead. In fact, it is widely believed that God Himself had a hand in the holy man's burial (DEUT. 34: 5,6).

⁵So Moses the servant of the Lord died there in the land of Moab, according to the word of the Lord, ⁶and he buried him in the valley in the land of Moab opposite Bethpeor; but no man knows the place of his burial to this day.

Perhaps the reason that God took the drastic measures of directing the burial of Moses Himself was because Satan was attempting to steal the body of Moses. This event is described in the letter of Jude verse nine.

⁹But when the archangel Michael, contending with the devil, disputed about the body of Moses, he did not presume to pronounce a reviling judgement upon him, but said, "The Lord rebuke you."

Jesus saw the ghosts of Moses and Elijah at the Transfiguration. Why did they appear? One belief is that they appeared for symbolic reasons. Moses represented the LAW and Elijah represented the PROPHETS in order to demonstrate that both the law and the prophets were validated in the coming of Jesus Christ.

Maybe He saw them simply because they were two of the most important personages of the Bible without any other reason needed.

Moses and Elijah talked with Jesus at great length during their visit with him, discussing primarily the upcoming trials that He was to endure and preparing Him for the new realm of existence into which He was about to enter.

The conclusion of the meeting was of a spectacular nature as the *shekinah* – the mighty cloud by which God often travelled - engulfed the mountaintop, terrifying the three apostles. The cloud was reminiscent of the one by which the Lord travelled during the time of the exodus (EXODOUS 40: 34-37).

[34]Then the cloud covered the tent of the meeting, and the glory of the Lord filled the tabernacle. [35]And Moses was not able to enter the tent of the meeting because the cloud abode upon it, and the glory of the Lord filled the tabernacle. [36]Throughout all their journeys, wherever the cloud was taken up over the tabernacle, the people of Israel would go onward; [37]but if the cloud was not taken up, then they did notgo onward until the day that it was taken up.

Thus, during the transfiguration, the cloud of the almighty could in a sense be considered a ghostly event in itself.

Witnesses are very important when considering the truthfulness of ghostly sightings. What better witnesses could one have than Jesus and his three most trusted disciples?

MARIAN SIGHTINGS

Just as there have been ghostly sightings of Jesus, there have also been sightings of His mother, Mary. Ghostly sightings of Mary present a particular problem because they have to be differentiated from Marian sightings of a purely visionary nature. And there is another mystery. When sightings are made of Mary – of any type – she is almost always floating in the air. An explanation for this will be made later.

Fatima and Lourdes are obvious examples of visionary events. Despite the huge crowds that attended these sightings the primary observers were limited to one person in each case. Bernadette was the only one who actually saw the Virgin Mary at Lourdes and Lucia was the only person who saw the actual figure of Mary at Fatima.

While other people took part in the two events as a whole, and some people claimed to see mists and strange lights, it was only the two girls who saw the figure of Mary and heard her voice. Fatima and Lourdes were the visions seen by two young girls and shared with the public.

During a typical ghostly sighting a number of people witness and sometimes also hear the spirit in question which generally does not deliver a prophetic message. Occasionally a family ghost will forewarn the doom of a particular family member or members. This is pretty much the extent of prognosticating ghosts.

An example of a ghost sighting of a Marian type would be the apparitions that were seen in Zeitoun, Egypt. The sightings began on April 2, 1968 and lasted until 1971. AT the time, Zeitoun was an economically underdeveloped suburb of Cairo and, although populated predominantly by Moslems, it has a large segment of people who belong to the Coptic Church. The Coptic Church is liturgically closely related to the Roman Catholic religion but, since breaking away has elected its own pope and maintains its own synod of bishops.

Zeitoun is particularly important because it is traditionally believed to be the site where Mary and Joseph took refuge with their child when fleeing Herod. An impressive Coptic church stands in Zeitoun and it is here that the sightings of Mary occurred.

The history of the church is of special interest. The ground on which it stands was donated to the Coptic Church in 1920 by the Khalil Ibrahim family. One of the members of the family had a dream in which the Virgin Mary appeared to him and asked that a church be built on the family property.

This dream was followed shortly by another one of even more profound content in which the Virgin Mary appeared again and announced that if the church was built she would appear on its rooftop in a year's time! This **is a very significant clue** to identify the sightings at Zeitoun as being of a ghostly nature.

The church was constructed in 1925. The Virgin Mary did not appear on the rooftop in a year's time however, she did appear **forty-two years later** in 1968. This is very consistent with ghostly activity. Ghosts frequently appear many years later than anticipated to fulfill a promise or to observe an anniversary. In fact, ghosts are notorious for showing up late.

Sometimes very late!

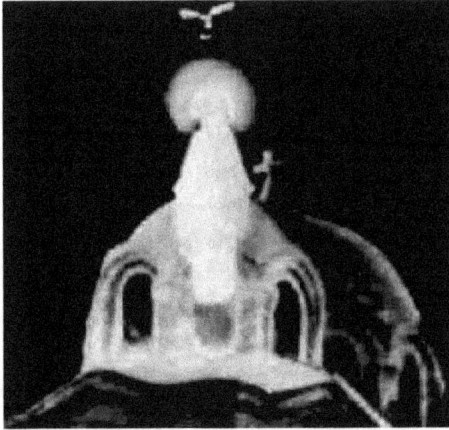

There are very many cases in which ghosts appear much later than expected and this is probably due to a very real time differential between the ghost's natural environment and the one into which it is to appear.

A prime example would be the ghost of Jasper Barker who appeared to his nephew Jasper Craven to inform him of a secret will he had written in which valuable property was left to the young would-be heir. The only problem is that the ghost appeared forty-four years after passing on and thus it was well beyond the statute of limitations deadline for probating a will.

Such seems the case for the ghost of Mary in Zeitoun. The ghost appeared on the rooftop as predicted but well past the predicted time.

The first sighting was made by two Moslem mechanics. They had taken a break one late night from their work in an automobile repair shop directly across the street from the Coptic Church. What they saw was a radiant figure strolling across the rooftop, accompanied by a small flock of luminous birds. Since the first sighting, the spirit of Mary continued to appear on a regular basis, usually sans birds.

The apparitions continued to occur for a couple of years and witnesses numbered in the many thousands. There are also many fine pictures of the sighting which was published in most of the worlds' newspapers.

And then as suddenly as the sightings began, they stopped. After nearly three years of rooftop appearances, the ghost of the Blessed Virgin did not appear again.

What to make of these sightings? The Catholic Church does not recognize them as true Marian visitations.

The question must be asked: was the woman on the rooftop truly the Virgin Mary? Maybe it was the ghost of another female. The spectre did not make any pronouncements or put forth any prophecies. It acted like any ghostly apparition. Whose ghost it truly was and why it appeared are still mysteries.

Sightings of the Virgin Mary are commonly airborne in nature. Another example of Mary being seen floating in the air was a sighting made in France in the year 1896. An unusual glow was noticed in the limbs of a large elm tree by a group of nuns who taught at a nearby parochial school. They went to investigate with several students.

Upon closer examination the glow clarified into the image of a young woman in a robe-like garment who fit the description of the Virgin Mary. In addition, other apparitions appeared in the vicinity of the elm tree. It was a frightful scene of demonic figures cavorting about in a hellish setting.

Similar to Zeitoun the appearance of this apparition was predicted. Fifty years earlier a local psychic prophesied that a ghostly manifestation would occur in the field near the school. And – like the Zeitoun event – this sighting occurred well after the predicted date, just as in the earlier noted much delayed appearances of expected ghost sightings.

The ghost that appeared in the elm tree looked like the Virgin Mary but did not identify itself or issue any prophecies or other warnings. As such, it would qualify as a ghost rather than a vision.

How to explain the two obvious similarities between the Zeitoun sightings and this sighting? Both events were predicted and the ghosts appeared belatedly.

Normally, such occurrences would be common features of what are known as urban legends which are stories of similar content that are a part of the folklore of several localities and usually contain a great deal of exaggeration.

But, due to the distance involved between the sightings - one in Egypt and the other in France - and because of the cultural differences of the observers, considering the two different sightings to be urban legends does not seem justified. Especially when both meet the criteria of common ghostly sightings.

The next Marian sighting occurred in Banneux, Belgium on January 15, 1933 and occurred in a little girl's back yard. The sighting revolves around three members of the Beco family: Mariette, her ten-year-old brother Julien, and their mother, Louise. Mariette was worried about her little brother who was late in arriving home. She repeatedly raised the bed

53

sheet that was placed over her window instead of a more expensive curtain to search for the arrival of Julien.

On one occasion she noticed something very unusual in the garden in her back yard. Standing amidst the winter shrubbery was the figure of a luminous young woman.

Mariette rushed into the kitchen to inform her mother about what she saw. Her mother nonchalantly told her that she'd probably seen a ghost. Mariette insisted that it was the Virgin Mary. The girl convinced her mother to come to the window and see for herself. Louise went to the bedroom window with her daughter and looked out into the garden where the figure still was.

Mariette's mother also saw the figure and was startled by it. She still thought that it was a ghost, even if it did look like the Virgin Mary. Mariette wanted to go outside for a closer look but her mother wouldn't allow this, and locked the door to keep her inside.

Marriette & Julien

After this initial sighting of the ghost of the Virgin Mary the event became greatly exaggerated and expanded into a full-fledged religious spectacle. However, the original apparition fits all the criteria for a ghostly sighting and once again the spirit is identified as the Virgin Mary.

A rooftop is once again the setting for the next sighting of the Virgin Mary. This occurred in Knock, Ireland on the night of August 21, 1879 in the County Mayo. It had rained all that day and the evening had become a dreary, atmospheric one where mists arose from the buildings and fields. Any type of illumination would be noticeable on an evening like this.

At about 8:15 PM three women were walking together down the streets of Knock and approached their local church. Upon the roof was a tableaux of Mary, Joseph and St. John. A mysterious illumination swirled about the religious figures and created a surreal scene. It became even more dreamlike when the three figures on the tableaux began to move!

Other passerby joined the three spectators and there was soon a large group of people viewing the ghostly scene. It began to lightly rain again. But the figures on the tableaux remained dry, looking even more phantasmagoric in the illuminated billowing mist. One of the onlookers rushed toward the image of the Virgin Mary to adore her but when she tried to grasp the figure by the feet her fingers gathered only air.

The figure of St. John was holding a Bible. The book was so real of appearance that the writing on the pages was visible and legible.

Eventually the group of figures started to slowly dissolve. They finally vanished entirely, leaving the tableaux in its original motionless condition after the brief period of animation.

Once more the sighting of the Virgin Mary was an airborne phenomenon. This occurs too frequently to be a mere coincidence. What does it mean? Why does Mary so often appear floating above the ground or on or near a rooftop?

Often the purpose of a ghostly visitation is to perform a re-enactment of a previous event. Maybe that's precisely what Mary's ghost is doing!

It is commonly believed that the Blessed Virgin Mary was bodily assumed into heaven rather than having to suffer a natural death. Is it possible that the ghostly sightings of her in the air are re-enactments of Mary in the process of rising up to heaven?

Ghostly events that are re-enactments usually involve a matter of great magnitude, something that would leave a lasting impression on someone. That is why it is replayed again and again. Rising bodily into heaven would certainly be an event of great magnitude!

But Mary arose into heaven at only one location. How is it that she is seen airborne at so many different places? Maybe the reason is because the area involved is the sky and the sky cannot truly be confined to any one specific location. The sky is in constant flux and a certain portion of it could be over Ireland at one time and over Israel at another.

Another way that Mary's ghost could be sighted at places where she may have never visited during her life time is by way of secondary contact. Secondary contact involves the passage of a relic of Mary or one of her possessions through an area which may later give rise to manifestations.

There is a third way that her ghost may be drawn to a location: by séance-like methods. Spirits of the deceased are called back to earth by mediums and through a séance so couldn't the ghost of Mary be likewise drawn to earth?

It wouldn't have to be a formal séance, but simply a devout believer in the Virgin Mary devoting an intense amount of effort and time to contacting her.

The last sighting of the Virgin Mary to be covered here is actually one of the first made. It occurred in 8th century England and involves a future saint and a bishop's swineherd named Oeves.

The future saint was a man named Egwin and he was in charge of a local parish. The land was still under the rule of the heathen Saxons and Egwin fought hard to get his parishioners to put aside their old pagan ways. His methods were so overbearing, however, that it caused disillusionment amongst his flock and the eventual loss of his parish.

Egwin felt that his parish had been unjustly taken from him by the bishop and set off for Rome to argue the matter before the pope. Before departing, he had himself bound in chains as a form of penance and he threw away the key to the padlock into the River Avon. Thus encumbered, the redoubtable Egwin made his way to Rome.

It was a tortuous trip during which Egwin starved himself. The papal attendants who met him at the gates to the city were so shocked by his emaciated appearance that they immediately had someone rush to the marketplace where a fish was purchased for him. Then an astounding thing happened. When the fish was gutted a key was found inside of it. It was the key to the padlock that Egwin had tossed into the Avon river!

When the pope heard of this he immediately had Egwin brought before him. God had clearly spoken in Egwin's favor. The pope ordered Egwin's parish returned to him.

But the story doesn't end here.   Egwin returned to England and he learned of a wondrous apparition that had occurred in his parish during his absence. The Virgin Mary had appeared in one of the fields near his church and had been seen by a swineherd named Oeves. Taking three companions with him, Egwin proceeded to the site of the apparition and he and the others saw the Virgin Mary, too.

This is all that is told of the story but it has been recorded as the oldest apparition of the Virgin Mary on record.

St. Egwin's

EZEKIEL'S SKELETONS

Ezekiel lived about 2,600 years ago during the height of the Babylonian Empire. He was the son of a high priest named Buzi and had been consecrated into the Zadokite priesthood himself. He became one of the major prophets during one of the dark periods of Israelite history. It was at the time when much of the Israelite population had been taken captive by the Babylonians. Ezekiel had also been taken captive and lived in exile in Telabib on the Chebar River which was also known as the "Grand Canal."

Ezekiel's life was uneventful until the age of thirty when he experienced the first of his many astonishing visions. Most people know of Ezekiel because of his two most famous visions; one in which he beheld the confounding wheels of light in the sky which were accompanied by bizarre alien beings and the other vision being the raising to life of the army of skeletons in the desert.

Ezekiel's life drastically changed with his first vision of the wheels and the strange beings. This was most likely a theophany – an event during which the nature of God is revealed. It's something that is best described by

Ezekiel himself: EZEKIEL 1: 15 – 19.

[15]Now as I looked at the living creatures, I saw a wheel upon the earth beside the living creatures, one four each of the four of them. [16]As for the appearance of the wheels and their construction: their appearance was like the gleaming of a chrysolite; and the four had the same likeness, their construction being as it were a wheel within a wheel. [17]When they went in any of their four directions without turning as they went. [18]The four wheels had rims and they had spokes; and their rims were full of eyes roundabout. [19]And when the living creatures went, the wheels went beside them; and when the living creatures rose from the earth, the wheels rose.

I don't know what Ezekiel saw. Some people claim these are extra-terrestrials and their aircraft. Some people claim that Ezekiel had seen either angels or demons. Others claim that he was having a psychotic hallucination or else one that was drug induced.

Still other people argue that there wasn't any one person named Ezekiel but that the book in the Bible that bears his name was actually written by several different people who'd lived between 586 BC and 230 BC.

The last theory is doubtful. Ezekiel's stories are too uniform in their telling and strange subject matter to have been written by more than one author. They came from a single mind.

Reading the spectacular events in the Book of Ezekiel is like reading a wildly imaginative science fiction novel. But his stories seem more real than fiction. Ezekiel lived in perilous and highly unusual times and he witnessed many extraordinary events that occurred because of the type of times in which he lived.

What about ghosts? More accurately – skeletons. It's a fascinating story that some biblical "authorities" attempted to change into a mundane, every day experience – explaining it as nothing more than a quaint allegory. Let's go directly to the words of Ezekiel and see how allegorical the event sounds: Ezekiel 37: 1-14.

As Ezekiel relates, the Hand of the Lord led him into a plain strewn with bones and the Lord conducted him through the bones which were dry and brittle from age. God asked the prophet if these dry, brittle bones could live. Ezekiel cautiously replied, "Oh Lord God, though knoweth."

God instructed Ezekiel: "Prophecy to these bones and say to them, 'Oh dry bones, hear the word of the Lord. Thus says the Lord God to these bones: behold, I will cause breath to enter you, and you shall live. And I will lay sinews upon you, and will cause flesh to come upon you, and cover you with skin, and put breath in you, and you shall live; and you shall know that I am Lord.'"

That is what God told Ezekiel to say to those bones in that dark and silent valley; and that is exactly what Ezekiel said to them. There was a loud rattling and crackling as the thousands upon thousands of bones began to stir in the dust and come together. All across the flat, desolate landscape bones now in the shape of men arose up and stretched out their arms and legs. Sinews grew onto the bones, and skin and flesh covered them. But the skeletons stood limp and lifeless because the breath of God had not been breathed into them yet.

Then the Lord instructed Ezekiel to say to the heavens: "Come from the four winds, Oh Breath, and breathe upon the slain, that they may live."

Ezekiel said the words and a great rush of wind swept the landscape and forced the breath of life into the skeletons, making them live again. The valley was filled with the army of former Israelite soldiers risen from the covering of dust in which it had lain.

This was a spectacle clearly described by Ezekiel. There were not any words of equivocation in his account, nothing to give the meaning of allegory. What Ezekiel described is what happened! The only allegory in this scene is what happens AFTER the bones are brought to life. AFTER. After the skeletons had been risen to life, God told Ezekiel that they represented the House of Israel as it would be taken up from the dust and made whole again. The rising up of the skeletons was real, what the act represented was the allegory.

It's clear from the words that Ezekiel used that he was describing an event as it was taking place. He didn't use qualifying words such as: AS IF or LIKE. Ezekiel did not say that the bones arose AS IF coming back to life and that they stood there LIKE the army of Israel animated again. No. He described the event as something taking place for real before his eyes. And that is exactly what it was. A field filled with skeletons that are once again clothed with flesh is certainly an impressive ghostly scene – one of the most powerful imaginable. And that is what Ezekiel saw!

LETTER FROM ELIJAH

Ghostly phenomenon of many types occur throughout the Bible, but it sometimes requires a great deal of tenacity to uncover them. A person also has to be able to recognize paranormal occurrences for what they are, which is not always easy. Such is the case with the delivery of a posthumous letter from the great prophet Elijah. It is one of the most extraordinary, yet least known, of all events in the Bible.

Elijah was one of those incredible figures from the Old Testament who seemed to perform miraculous feats on an almost daily basis. More than once did he raise a person from the dead. One occasion is described in 1 KINGS 17:21,22.

[21]Then he stretched himself upon the child three times, and cried to the Lord, "Oh Lord my God, let this child's soul come into him." [22]And the Lord hearkened to the voice of Elijah; and the soul ofthe child came into him again, and he revived.

Elijah had many supernatural experiences, many of which were unique. On one occasion he spoke directly to the voice of God which issued to him from the depths of a cave. Another time Elijah was fed by ravens when he couldn't get food for himself. And of course, Elijah was one of the few people who did not officially die and was taken up to heaven in a fiery chariot. This event was described in 2 KINGS 2: 9-12.

[9]When they had crossed Elijah said to Elisha, "Ask what I shall do for you, before I am taken up from you." And Elisha said, "I pray you, let me inherit a double share of your spirit." [10]And he said, "You have asked a hard thing; yet if you see me as I am being taken from you, it shall be so for you; but if you do not see me, it shall not be so." [11]And as they still went on and talked, behold, a chariot of fire and horses of fire separated the two of them. And Elijah went up by a whirlwind into heaven. [12]And Elisha saw it and cried, "My father, my father! The chariots of Israel and its horsemen!" And he saw him no more.

Being taken directly into heaven without having to die is a rare event, but even in Elijah's time there had already been one precedent: Enoch. Genesis 5: 22-24.

[22]Enoch walked with God after the birth of Methuselah three

hundred years, and had other sons and daughters. [23]Thus all the days of Enoch were three hundred and sixty-five years. [24]Enoch walked with God; and he was not, for God took him.

God had a particular liking for Enoch and wanted his company in heaven and so he took him from the face of the earth. Enoch is also famous for a book he'd written which revealed many occult secrets and wonders.

Elijah is also well known for a book, which is his entry into the Old Testament. He is less known, however, for having had a letter posthumously delivered to a king of Judah named Jehoram. This particular Jehoram was the son of Jehosaphat and took over the reign of Judah upon his father's death.

He is not to be confused with the many other Jehoram's in extant at that time. It apparently was an exceptionally popular name around 845 B.C.. Jehoram had a brother-in-law named Jehoram and Jehoram was also the name of the king of Israel which was a separate kingdom from Judah at this period.

Jehoram of Judah was the first-born son of Jehosaphat and as such was in place to be the seventh king in the Davidic line. Nonetheless, he was determined to eliminate ANY possible threat to his rule so, upon attaining the kingship, he ordered the execution of all of his brothers.

This made God quite angry with him. What also made God very angry was Jehoram's forsaking the laws of his fathers and the setting up of foreign gods before his people. In addition to this he was a cruel and brutal person who was despised by everyone. His was a wicked rule which spanned the years 848 B.C. to 841 B.C. and which came to a slow, agonizing end as warned by Elijah.

The warning came to Jehoram just after he'd put down a revolt by the Edomites. It was a prophecy given to him in writing by Elijah. Elijah had been taken up into heaven on the fiery whirlwind about four years previous to this, so the fact that Jehoram received a letter from the "departed" prophet was at the very least a curious thing.

The Bible isn't clear as to who actually presented the document to Jehoram, but it is VERY CLEAR that it came from Elijah. Again, it isn't certain whether Elijah made a special appearance on earth to give the letter to Jehoram – which seems unlikely: why not just tell him the prophecy? – or if he had given it to someone else to deliver the letter. While this may not be certain, what is certain is that the prophecy was delivered AFTER Elijah had been translated into heaven. Was it shock or cynical disbelief with which Jehoram read the message which is described in 2 Chronicles 21:

12-15?

[12]And a letter came to him from Elijah the prophet, saying, "Thus says the Lord, the God of David your father. 'Because you have not walked in the ways of Jehosaphat your father, or in the ways of Asa king of Judah, [13] but have walked in the way of the kings of Israel, and have led Judah and the inhabitants of Jerusalem into unfaithfulness, and also you have killed your brothers, of your father's house, who were better than yourself; [14]behold, the Lord will bring a great plague on your people, your children, your wives, and all your possessions, [15]and you yourself will have a severe sickness with a disease of your bowels, until your bowels come out because of the disease, day by day.'"

Soon after Jehoram received this direful warning, the Philistines joined forces with the Arabs and invaded Judah. Jehoram's army was decimated. His wives, possessions and sons were taken from him with the exception of Jehoahaz who escaped with his father. But Jehoram could not escape the disease which overcome him and left him in constant agony as his bowels seeped from his body day by day. He lingered for two years before death freed him.

No one mourned Jehoram's death and he was not placed on the holy pyre reserved for great leaders. But because he was of the line of David, Jehoram was buried in the city of David but not among the great kings.

It all came to pass as Elijah had prophesied, this time proving his great abilities from beyond this world.

The Bridge to Hell

There are many near-death experiences recorded in the Bible in both the Old and the New Testament. These occurred during the many occasions in which an individual was raised from the dead by either Jesus or a saint or a prophet.

Did those people risen from the dead have near-death experiences to talk about? They probably did, although these experiences aren't discussed in the pages of the Bible.

It shouldn't make any difference by what mechanism these resurrected people were brought to life insofar as the type of near-death experience they might have had. It doesn't matter HOW a person came back from the dead – just that he DID!

There is a phrase that is used repeatedly throughout the Bible which bears upon the study of ghosts which it would be important to examine here. The phrase is: giving up the ghost. It is meant to describe the release through the final breath of a dying person the spirit that had animated the body. This escaping spirit was obviously seen – both in reality and figuratively – as a ghost departing the body.

The term, giving up the ghost, is a description used frequently in the Bible and is closely associated specifically with the Scriptures. Why would this term be so widely used if it wasn't meant to be seriously taken? Giving up the ghost. Freeing the spirit of the soul from its bodily confines. The word ghost is a perfect description of this event.

What happens if the body of the person who'd given up the ghost is revived? Can the ghost return to the body? There is the description of such an event in 1 Kings 17: 17-22. It involves an account of Elijah – Elijah again – raising back to life the son of a widow.

[17]And it came to pass after these things, that the son of the woman, the mistress of the house fell sick; and his sickness was so sore, that there was no breath left in him. [18]And she said unto Elijah, "What have I to do with thee, Oh thou man of God? Art thou come unto me to call my sin to

remembrance, and to slay my son?" [19]And he said unto her, "Give me thy son." And he took him out of her bosom, and carried him up into the loft, and laid him upon his own bed. [20]And cried unto the Lord, and said, "Oh Lord my God, hast thou also brought evil upon the widow with whom I sojourn, by slaying her son? [21]And he stretched himself upon the child three times, and cried unto the Lord, and said, "Oh Lord my God I pray thee, let this child's soul come back into him again." [22]And the Lord heard the voice of Elijah; and the soul of the child came back into him again, and he revived.

Elisha – who might be considered Elijah's replacement - was involved in the following resuscitation, but not until after he'd dispatched an apprentice to attempt the feat first. A young child had gone out to the field in search of his father, but soon returned home complaining of an agonizing headache. His mother took him into her arms to comfort him, but the child shortly died.

Laying her son in a protected place, the distraught mother hurriedly saddled a donkey and rode the rugged fifteen miles to where Elisha was staying. Elisha listened to her story but instead of travelling with her to where her dead son lay he sent his servant, Gehazi. It isn't explained why

Elisha didn't go himself. At any rate, Gehazi was unable to bring life back to the boy so he disconsolately rode back to Elisha to give him the sad news.

Elisha had to tend to the matter himself. He promptly rode to the Shunammite woman's home, and what happened then is described in 2 Kings 4:32-35.

³²When Elisha came into the house, he saw the child lying dead on his bed. ³³So he went in and shut the door upon the two of them, and prayed to the Lord. ³⁴Then he went up and laid upon the child, putting his mouth upon his mouth, his eyes upon his eyes, and his hands upon his hands: and as he stretched himself upon him, the flesh of the child became warm. ³⁵Then he got up again, and walked once to and fro in the house, and went up, and stretched himself upon him; the child sneezed seven times, and the child opened his eyes.

There's much more to the story than this and it occurs before the birth of the boy that had been risen from the dead. There was a time when the boy's mother had not been able to bear children. She knew Elisha then from his constant travels throughout the barren countryside. Out of kindness, she and her husband set up a special room where the holy man could stop and rest during his gruelling trips.

Moved by their kindness, Elisha asked them if there was anything he could do for them. They did not need any material comforts because they were wealthy, but the one thing they wanted they had been denied – a child! The great prophet assured them that within a year's time they would have a son in their home. They did. The son was the same boy that Elisha was later to raise from the dead.

Elisha was a man of such power that he was even responsible for raising a person from the dead – after HE HIMSELF had died. Ironically, for the great personage that Elisha was, his own death was very ordinary, unlike Elijah's. Although, maybe Elisha's timing could be considered extraordinary. He died just moments after delivering a final, glorious prophecy to Joash, the then reigning king of Israel. This is how it was described in 2 Kings 13: 15-20.

[15]And Elisha said to him, "Take a bow and arrows;" so he took a bow and arrows. [16]Then he said to the king of Israel, "Draw the bow;" and he drew it. And Elisha laid his hands upon the king's hands. [17]And he said, "Open the window eastward;" and he opened it. Then Elisha said, "Shoot;" and he shot. And he said, "The Lord's arrow of victory, the

arrow of victory over Syria! For you have to fight the Syrians in Aphek until you have made an end of them." [18]And he said, "Take the arrows;" and he took them. And he said to the king of Israel, "Strike the ground with them;" and he struck three times and stopped. [19]Then the man of God was angry with him, and said, "You should have struck five or six times; then you would have struck down Syria until you had made an end of it, but now you will strike down Syria only three times." [20]So Elisha died, and they buried him.

So Elisha died, and they buried him. Could there have been a more simple epitaph for such a great personage? So Elisha died, and they buried him?

Even in death he was a powerful man! Just touching the bones of this mighty prophet could bring about miracles, as is written in 2 Kings 13: 21.

[21]And as a man was being buried, lo, a marauding band was seen and the man was cast into the grave of Elisha; and as soon as the man touched the bones of Elisha, he revived, and stood on his feet.

An interesting scene: a funeral party tossing the corpse into an open grave upon sight of the approach of a band of raiders. Of course, that was followed by an even more interesting sight: the corpse leaping on its own out of the grave! Just being in the proximity of Elisha's bones gave life back to the dead man.

Tradition states that the revived man lived for only another hour. What might he have done in that extra allotted time?

Raisings from the dead occurred in the New Testament as well as the Old. Most people are familiar with the times when Jesus raised people from the dead, particularly the story of Lazarus. But how many people remember the time when Jesus passed through the town of Nain and raised a widow's son back to life as told in Luke 6: 12-15?

[12]As he drew near to the gate of the city, behold a man who had died was being carried out, the only son of his mother, and she was a widow; and a large crowd from the city was with her. [13]And when the Lord saw her, he had compassion on her and said to her, "Do not weep." [14]And he came and touched the bier, and the bearers stood still. And he said to him, "Young man, I say to you, arise." [15]And the dead man sat up, and began to speak. And he gave him to his mother.

Notice how once again the person being raised back to life is a widow's only surviving son. In both the Old and the New Testament there is a decided proclivity for the sons of widows to be chosen for resurrection from the dead. The obvious reason would be because an aging widow would be in more desperate need of the help of a son than anyone else.

Both Paul and Peter are credited with having raised people from the dead. A female disciple named Dorcas-Tabitha was one of those who'd been risen. The woman had two first names because during that period it was common for Jews to adopt two names – one Hebrew and the other either Greek or Latin. This explains why later Peter refers to her by both names.

While peter was en route to a town called Joppa he learned of the death of this beloved female disciple and hurried to her side. Friends of the deceased rushed upon the apostle, beseeching him to pray over her. What then happened is described in Acts 9: 39-41.

[39]So Peter rose and went with them. And when he had come, they took him to the upper room. All the widows stood beside him, weeping, and showing coats and garments which Dorcas made while she was with

them. [40]But Peter put them all outside and knelt down and prayed; then turning to the body he said, "Tabitha, rise." And she opened her eyes, and when she saw Peter she sat up. [41]And he gave her his hand and lifted her up. Then calling the saints and widows he presented her alive.

Paul also had the ability to raise the dead back to life. The following story would be humorous if it wasn't so tragic.

Paul was known as a powerful speaker. Sometimes his talks went on at great length, and sometimes too long for the younger listeners in his audience.

During one of Paul's sermons one of the younger members of the group, named Eutychus, settled down to rest on the ledge of an upper story windowsill, leaning back against the frame of the opened window. Because Paul's talk was exceptionally long this evening, Eutychus dozed off in his comfortable spot. While Paul was still speaking, the young boy fell out the window and slammed to the ground. What occurred was described in Acts 20: 7-12.

[7]On the first day of the week, when we were gathered together to break bread, Paul talked with them, intending to depart on the morrow; and

he prolonged his speech until midnight. [8]There were many lights in the upper chamber where we were gathered. [9]And a young man named Eutychus was sitting in the window. He sank into a deep sleep as Paul talked still longer; and being overcome by sleep, he fell down from the third story and was taken up dead. [10]But Paul went down and bent over him, and embracing him said, "Do not be alarmed, for his life is in him." [11]And when Paul had gone up and broken bread and eaten, he conversed with them for a long while, until daybreak, and so departed. [12]And they took the lad away live, and were not a little comforted.

It isn't mentioned whether or not Eutychus attended any more of Paul's sermons. Nor is it ever revealed whether or not Eutychus suffered from narcolepsy, the condition in which a person spontaneously drops into a sound slumber.

Did Eutychus experience a near death event as have so many people who'd "given up the ghost" for a temporary period? And if he had – would it have been similar to contemporary near death experiences or did people in biblical times go through a different type of near death experience?

Why would their near death experience be different? Consider the basic phenomena of a contemporary near death event: travel down a lengthy tunnel toward an increasingly brighter white light at the end of which stands the figure of Jesus or a Christ like figure. But could this have happened during the time of Jesus?

Take into account a person who'd been raised from the dead by Jesus Himself. Who would the raised person encounter at the end of the tunnel? Jesus? But if it had been Jesus who'd just raised him from the dead what then! Imagine the confusion.

Not only that: could Jesus be in two places at the same time? Could Jesus have stood at both ends of the tunnel that extends between the realms of life and death at the same time, assuming that while on earth he was an ordinary man?

While still considering raisings from the dead during biblical times as opposed to those of contemporary times it is important to note that they differ in one extremely vital point – the time lapse in between. In the biblical cases it is common for the person who'd been brought back to life to have been deceased for an hour or longer, usually days. It is certainly miraculous for a person who'd been deceased that long to resume normal activity. This does not occur in contemporary times.

What this means is that the biblical raisings from the dead would be more likely to produce ghosts because of the length of time in which the deceased spirit was kept out of the body.   What kind of experiences did these people have while deceased?   Did they spend time in heaven?   Did they spend time in hell?   Purgatory?   Limbo?   Or did their ghosts wander aimlessly through the ether.

Many of these people who'd came back from the dead came back with fascinating stories to tell.

JOSHUA'S SPECTRAL VISITANT

What type of being was it that Joshua encountered atop the hill outside of Jericho prior to the taking of that city?   The Israelites had just crossed the Jordan River and the males had undergone mass circumcision to remove the reproach of Egypt during which time this important religious ritual had been forbidden.   Now Joshua – new leader of the Israelites – prepared to assault Jericho.   As he surveyed the surroundings, a spectral visitor appeared(Joshua 5: 13-15).

[13] When Joshua was by Jericho, he lifted up his eyes and looked, and behold, a man stood before him with his drawn sword in his hand; and Joshua went to him and said to him, "Are you for us, or for our

adversaries?" [14] And he said, "No; but as commander of the army of the Lord I have now come." And Joshua fell on his face to the earth, and worshipped, and said, "What does my lord bid his servant?" And the commander of the Lord's army said to Joshua, "Put off your shoes from your feet; for the place where you stand is holy." And Joshua did so.

Who was this mysterious visitor? Most people immediately assume it's the Archangel Michael because the martial being with sword in hand seems to fit the usual description of Michael, the battling angel. But nowhere in this passage is the spirit described as Michael or even as an angel. This is extremely odd if the strange visitor was Michael the Archangel because in the Bible when an angel is the subject of activity it is almost always announced as such. Angels do not keep their identity secret for long.

Some people claim that Joshua's visitor is Jesus. The wording in the passage alone makes this identification highly unlikely. Would Jesus refer to himself as: "…commander of the army of the lord…"? This seems quite redundant.

Other people claim that the visitor is God Himself. But then, there's the same problem with the wording in the passage – redundancy!

And also, again, when God is speaking He lets you know right off that it's Him. God doesn't play guessing games in the pages of the Bible.

So who is Joshua's mysterious visitor? It seems to be a disembodied spirit of some form whose true purpose was to give Joshua confidence. A ghostly type of prophetic being. Is this the type of being whom Saul had been trying to find so long ago when he visited the Witch of Endor – a being that could tell him the future and give him strength?

Is this also the same being who also visited Daniel centuries after the visitation with Joshua? Like Joshua, Daniel was standing alone minding his own business when he was suddenly visited by a spectral being who did not identify himself. Additionally, this being was certainly neither Jesus nor God as shown in Daniel 10: 4-7.

[4]On the twenty-fourth day of the first month, as I was standing on the bank of the great river, that is, the Tigris, [5]I lifted up my eyes and looked, and beheld, a man clothed in linen, whose loins were girded with gold of Uphaz. [6]His body was like beryl, his face like the appearance of lightning, his arms and legs like the gleam of burnished bronze, and the sounds of his wordslike the noise of a multitude.

That this being has come to bear a prophecy is made certain. Also certain is that it is not God, Jesus or the Archangel Michael because of its limitations (Daniel 10: 13, 14).

[13]The prince of the kingdom of Persia withstood me twenty-one days; but Michael, one of the chief princes, came to help me, so I left him there with the prince of the Kingdom of Persia [14]and came to make you understand what is to befall your people in the later days. For the vision is for days yet to come.

Could this apparition be a type of family ghost? Family ghosts are well recorded throughout history and usually appear for the specific purpose of prophecy. Inasmuch as Joshua and Daniel do hail from the same racial family it would only seem to make sense that they would be visited by the same family ghost bearing prophecy. It would not be unusual.

VOICES FROM SHEOL

Isaiah was the son of Amoz. Isaiah prophesied under five kings of Judah and had access to the royal court at Jerusalem where he was at one time the advisor to King Hezekiah.

He began his career as a prophet in 740 B.C. and continued until the reign of the wicked King Manasseh during which Isaiah suffered martyrdom by being sawn asunder. It was through the supplication of Isaiah in about 701 B.C. that God devastated the attacking Sennacherib army of 185,000 men, scattering the remains of the army back to Nineveh.

Isaiah is well known for the many spectacular prophecies he made that were fulfilled, including: the fall of Babylon, the restoration of Israel and the establishment of the second Jewish Nation in the Promised Land.

The prophecy of current interest is the fall of Babylon which has already been touched upon during the examination of the ghostly handwriting on the wall. But there are even more supernatural events connected with the fall of Babylon, an event that Isaiah predicted two centuries before it occurred.

Babylon was one of the first great civilizations of humankind. This is why it is of such importance.

Ancient Babylon was founded by Nimrod who was a great-grandson of Noah. The Amorites were the first people to rule Babylon at around 1760 B.C. and were ruled by the great lawgiver, Hammurabi.

The Hittites took over from the Amorites around 760 B.C. and they were in turn overthrown by the Chaldeans who were led by the famous Nebuchadnezzar. It was about this time that the Israelites were conquered and forced into the period of the so-called Babylon captivity. This ended with the fall of Babylon when the Persians and Medes attacked under Cyrus, an event foretold by the handwriting on the wall.

As already mentioned, Isaiah predicted the fall of Babylon two centuries before it occurred. And his description of the event was directly to the point. He wasn't just guessing, as can be seen in verses four through nine in chapter 22 as Isaiah described Balshazzar's feast while the enemy is at the gate.

[4]My mind reels, horror has appalled me; the twilight I longed for has been turned for me into trembling. [5]They prepare the table, they spread the

rugs, they eat, they drink, arise, oh princes, oil the shield. He goes on further: [6]For thus the Lord said to me: "Go, set a watchman, let him announce what he sees. [7]When he sees riders, horsemen in pairs, riders on asses, riders on camels, let him listen diligently, very diligently." [8]Then he who saw cried: "Upon a watchtower I stand, oh Lord, continually by day, and at my post I am stationed whole nights. [9]And behold, here come riders, horsemen in pairs!" And he answered, "Fallen, fallen is Babylon: and all the images of her gods he has shattered to   the ground."

Isaiah continues:

[14]"Assemble, all of you, and hear!   Who among them has declared these things?   The Lord loves him: he shall perform his purpose on Babylon, and his arm shall be against the Chaldeans. [15]I even I, have spoken and called him, I have brought him, and he will prosper in his way.

This is where the ghosts come in. In chapter fourteen, verses eight through eleven, Isaiah describes a horrific scene at the gates of hell(?) as the king of Babylon enters this realm (actually called Sheol which is not truly hell). Sheol is described in the Bible as a type of hellish waiting area where spirits are held until a final judgment. Babylon's king had just been killed at the fall of the city and was being taunted by the ghosts of slain kings of the past.

[8]The cypress rejoices at you, the cedars of Lebanon, saying, 'Since you were laid low, no hewer comes up against us.' [9]'Sheol beneath is stirred up to meet you when you come, it rouses the shades to greet you, all who were leaders of the earth; it raises from their thrones all who were kings of the nations. [10]All of them will speak and say to you: 'You too have become weak as we! You have become like us!' [11]Your pomp is brought down to Sheol, the sound of your harps; maggots are the bed beneath you, and worms are your covering.

Only poetic writing? Taking account the many prophecies of Isaiah's that came to pass and that were written in poetic form, could one say the same thing about the references to Sheol? It would imply that Isaiah also possessed a special insight into the nether land, the land of Sheol, and the happenings there. Only poetic writing? Or prophecy in poetic form?

FAMILIAR SPIRITS

Familiar spirits can be described as any type of paranormal entity that a witch, wizard, sorceress, or other wielder of magical powers conjures up to help carry out his or her nefarious schemes. Sometimes they're cats. Sometimes they're mice. They might be frogs or goats or spiders or sometimes even creatures of indefinite nature.

Are familiar spirits merely the products of fairy tales and imagination? Not according to the Bible. Familiar spirits are another form of supernatural entity which the Bible treats as real. If familiar spirits were purely imaginary why would the Bible spend so much effort warning people not to deal with them! Not only are warnings given, but consequences, too, as in Leviticus 20: 27.

[27] A man or a woman that hath a familiar spirit, or that is a wizard, shall surely be put to death...

A warning was also given in Leviticus 19:31.

[31]Regard not them that have familiar spirits, neither seek after wizards.

The long litany cautioning against having dealings with familiar sprits is continued in Deuteronomy 18: 10, 11.

[10] There shall not be found among you any one that maketh his son or daughter to pass through the fire, or that useth divination, or an observer of times, or an enchanter, or a witch, [11]or a charmer, or a consulter with familiar spirits, or a wizard or a necromancer.

If these types of people did not exist and were not imbued with some form of power why would the Bible guard against them?

King Manasseh was reviled in the Bible for forcing the Hebrew people to accept idolatry and sorcery. He began his reign when but twelve-years-old, participating in a co-regency with Hezekiah. Manasseh specifically re-introduced Assyrian-Chaldean star worship, accepting the blood lusting female deity Astarte as high goddess. From 2 Kings 21:6:

[6]And he made his son pass through the fire, and observed times, and used enchantments, and dealt with familiar spirits and wizards...

It was said that Manasseh had more pagan gods before him than even the heathen Canaanites, which was a striking statement since the Canaanites were usually considered the worst of the worst when considering pagan beliefs.

Not only did Manasseh restore idolatry, call upon familiar spirits and use astrologers, he even re-introduced human sacrifice which is what is meant by the statement, "...made his son pass through the fire..." Manasseh was also the one who had the great prophet Isaiah sawed in two.

A massive reform campaign had to be instituted following the reign of Manasseh. A new covenant with God was devised and all of the idols and other effects of Manasseh's pagan regime had to be destroyed as outlined in 2 Kings 23:4-6.

[4]And the king commanded Hilkiah, the high priest and the priests of the second order, and the keepers of the threshold, to bring out of the temple of the Lord all of the vessels made for Baal, for Asherah, and for all the host of heaven; he burned them outside Jerusalem in the fields of Kidron, and carried their ashes to Bethel. [5]And he deposed the idolatrous priests whom the king of Judah had ordained to burn incense in the high places at

the cities of Judah and round about Jerusalem; those also who burned incense to Baal, to the sun, and the moon, and the constellations and all the hosts of heaven. [6]And he brought out the Asherah from the house of the Lord, outside Jerusalem, to the brook of Kidron, and burned it at the brook Kidron, and beat it to dust and cast the dust of it upon the graves of common people.

The destruction of the profane relics goes on for quite a lengthy stretch and in graphic detail, demonstrating how deeply the new heathenism of Manasseh had bored into the soul of Israel.

Witchcraft and familiar spirits were also seen to be a great problem during more modern times as well. The original Puritans in America had their run in with the problem and, although having certainly gotten far out of control in regard to the witch hunts, the pronouncements against familiars were based on words from the Bible.

Cotton Mather was a famous Puritan leader who was well known for being able to "discover" witches and root out familiar spirits. A section from one of his most famous works, *Wonders of the Invisible World,* demonstrates in detail how to deal with a familiar spirit when one is suspected to be about.

The Night after, the child fell into strange and sad fits, wherein it continued for Divers Weeks.   One Doctor Jacob advised her to hang up the Child's blanket, in the chimney Corner all Day, and at Night, when she went to put the child into it, she found any Thing in it then to throw it without fear into the fire.   Accordingly, at Night, there fell a great Toad out of the Blanket, which ran up and down the Hearth.   A boy catch'it, and held it in the fire with Tongs: where it made a horrible Noise,and flashd like Gunpowder, with a report like that of a Pistol: whereupon the Toad was nowhere to be seen.   The next Day a Kinswoman of Duny's told the Deponent, that her aunt was all griveously scorch'd with the Fire, and the deponent going to her House, found her in such a condition.   Duny told her, she might thank her for it; but she should live to see some of her Children Dead, and herself upon crutches.   But after the burning of the Toad, this Child Recovered.

There are occasions, it is said by Mather, when ghosts are used as a type of familiar as is also stated in his book *Wonders of the Invisible World.*

It has been a frequent thing for Bewitched People to be entertained with Apparitions of Ghosts of Murdered People, at the same time that the Spectres of the Witches troubled them. These Ghosts do always affright the Beholders more than all the other spectral Representations; and when they exhibit themselves, they cry out of being Murthered by the witch-crafts or other Violences of the Person who are then in spectre present.

In the above case not only is the murder victim's ghost present but so too is the ghost of the witch that perpetrated the murder.

A final point about familiar spirits: they can be bequeathed to a witch's or wizard's children upon death, assuming of course that the children wish to possess them.

Noting all of the havoc that can be spread by familiar spirits, it appears that there is good reason why the Bible speaks out so loudly against them. A person may want to have second thoughts about accepting one that may have been left to him by a friend or relative.

LYING SPIRITS

Has God ever used false prophets – so-called lying spirits – for His own purposes? Yes. Although there aren't many instances of this happening there are a few recorded in the Bible where this has occurred.

The first account is in 1 KINGS and took place during the time when rule of the Chosen People was divided between Jehoshaphat in Judah and Ahab in Israel. Syria was a nearby neighbor and there had been three years of peace between that land and Israel but Ahab was unhappy about the fact that one of his cities – Ramoth-Gilead – was still in the possession of the Syrian king, Benhadad. Ramoth-Gilead had been one of the most important cities belonging to the tribe of Gad and Ahab was anxious for its return, a matter which he discussed with Jehoshaphat.

Jehoshaphat's advice was to consult the Lord and to get as much advice as possible. Thus as many as four hundred prophets were summoned to give their opinions and they all had the same advice: go to war with Syria. Jehoshaphat was very suspicious about this result, knowing that it's almost impossible to get four hundred people to all agree on anything.   So he asked Ahab, "Is there not one other man of whom we may inquire?"

Ahab's response was direct: "There is yet one man of whom we may inquire of the Lord, Micaiah the son of Imlah; but I hate him, for he never prophecies good concerning me, but evil."

Jehoshaphat insisted, however, and Micaiah – not to be confused with the more famous prophet named Micah – was summoned. When questioned about the advisability of doing battle for the city of Ramoth-Gilead, Micaiah replied, "I saw all Israel scattered upon the mountains, as sheep that have no shepherd; and the Lord said, 'these have no master; let each return to his home in peace.'"   This prompted Ahab to say to Jehoshaphat, "Did I not tell you that he would not prophesy good concerning me, but evil?"

But Micaiah had much more to say as can be seen in 1 Kings 22: 19-23.

[19]And Micaiah said, "Therefore, hear the word of the Lord: I saw the Lord sitting on his throne, and all the host of heaven standing beside him on his right hand and on his left; [20]and the Lord said, 'Who will entice Ahab, that he may go up and fall at Ramoth-Gilead?'   And one said one thing, and

another said another. [21]Then a spirit came forward and stood before the Lord, saying, 'I will entice him.' [22]And the Lord said to him, 'By what means?' And he said, 'I will go forth and be a lying spirit in the mouth of all his prophets.' And he said, 'You are to entice him, and you shall succeed; go forth and do so.' [23]Now therefore behold, the Lord has put a lying spirit in the mouth of all these your prophets; the Lord has spoken evil concerning you."

Based on Micaiah's words it appears that God polled the various spirits around him and one spirit came forward and agreed to make liars out of the prophets in question. As a result this lying spirit did as planned and the four hundred prophets declared that to attack Syria would be a beneficial venture and that Ramoth-Gilead would be successful.

Micaiah, however, warned that such an attack would lead to Ahab's death and leave his people leaderless and floundering. And this is what happened.

There was another event in history whose outcome was dictated by the advice of evil spirits. It concerned Abimelech and divine vengeance turned upon him for his ordering the massacre of the 70 sons of Jerubaal to gain rule over Israel (Judges 9: 22-24).

[22]Abimelech ruled over Israel three years. [23]And God sent an evil spirit between Abimelech and the men of Shechem; and the men of Shechem dealt treacherously with Abimelech; [24]That the violence done to the seventy sons of Jerubaal might come and their blood be laid upon Abimelech their brother, who slew them, and upon the men of Shechem, who strengthened his hands to slay his brothers.

And evil spirits continue in this vein into more modern times, not confining their activities to the ancient days of the Old Testament. Cotton Mather was careful to document such matters and in his book *Wonders of the Invisible World* brings under examination a case of familiar spirits dating to the year 858 A.D..

...a certain Pestilent and Malignant type of Daemon, molested Caumont in Germany with all sorts of methods to stir up strife among the Citizens. He uttered Prophecies, he detected Villanies, he branded people with all forms of Infamies. He incensed the neighbourhood against one Man particularly, as the cause of the mischiefs; who yet proved himself innocent. He threw stones at the Inhabitants, and at length burnt their

Habitations, till the Commission of the Daemon could go no further...

While this spirit demonstrates the behaviors of a typical poltergeist it seems to be too direct of purpose with a specific plan in mind to be a simple poltergeist (if there is such a thing as a *simple* poltergeist). It prophesied and accused people of crimes. Although this story is not taken from the Bible and the spirit involved does not seem to have been dispatched by God, it acts with specific intent, demonstrating a conscious entity behind the actions. A curious event in history whose ultimate meaning and purpose is still a mystery.

JOB SEES A GHOST

In the Book of Job there is a very intriguing question about a brief glimpse that this great Biblical writer had of a ghostly form. Nothing more needs to be added to the beautifully brief passage and it is here in full as follows (Job 4: 12-19):

[12]"Now a word was brought to me stealthily, my ear received the whisper of it. [13]Amid thoughts from visions of the night when deep sleep falls on men, [14]dread came upon me, and trembling, which made all my bones shake. [15]A spirit glided past my face; the hair of my flesh stood up. [16]A form was before my eyes; there was silence then I heard a voice: [17]can mortal man be righteous before God? Can a man be pure before his Maker? [18]Even in his servants he puts no trust, and his angels he charges with error; [19]how much more those who dwell in houses of clay, whose foundation is in the dust, who are crushed before the moth. (underline my own).

Basically, Job is relating how a ghost appeared to him at bedtime and briefly spoke to him on religious matters. A fascinating little story from the Bible where ghosts once again appear quite real.

KEEPERS OF THE THRESHOLD

The entrance to a building can be a very dangerous place. Any building. But particularly a building of religious use. Why? Because it is here that evil spirits and other spirits intent on causing trouble seek to perform their most wicked deeds for the simple reason that the structure represents concepts contrary to their nature. Evil often attempts to battle its opposite force wherever it finds it.

It is widely known that especially the thresholds of ordinary homes need protection as can be demonstrated by the common practice in the Middle Ages of placing bay leaves under the threshold of the entrance to the house. This was to keep witches and their familiars from entering the building. It was believed that witches and their servants could not cross a threshold that is protected by bay leaves.

And what about vampires? They are usually associated with evil. Their entrance into the home or other places is thwarted by the strategic placing of garlic at various locations.

The Great Temple of Jerusalem like any other building also required protection of its various entrances from evil beings. As a result the office of Keepers of the Threshold was instituted. Their responsibility was to prevent entrance into the Temple by all unauthorized persons, both human and nonhuman.

The thresholds of the Great Temple were also the separation points between other-dimensional domains, the boundary between earthly existence and other realms. It was vitally important to guard these access points against the entrance of evil forces.

Taking this concept even further: the entrances to towns and cities also needed protection from supernatural encroachment. In the Hebrew religion during biblical times the office of Gatekeeper was given the responsibility of guarding these locations. Gatekeepers were basically the first line of defense and occupied a lesser rank than the Keepers of the Threshold.

Keepers of the Threshold were major figures in the Hebrew religion. Their office extends far back into the earliest days of the people of Israel. The lineage of this important office is fully described in 1 Chronicles 9: 17-27.

[17]The gatekeepers were: Shallum, Akkub, Talmon, Ahiman and their kinsmen (Shallum being the chief), [18]stationed hitherto in the king's gate on the east side. These were the gatekeepers of the camp of the Levites. [19]Shallum the son of Kore, son of Ebiasaph, son of Korah, and his kinsman of his father's house, the Korahites, were in charge of the work of the service, keepers of the threshold of the tent, as their fathers had been in charge of the camp of the Lord, keepers of the entrance. [20]And Phinehas the son of Eleazar was the ruler over them in time past; the Lord was with him. [21]Zechariah the son of Meshel-emiah was the gatekeeper at the entrance of the tent of meeting. [22]All these, who were chosen as gatekeepers at the thresholds, were two hundred and twelve. They were enrolled by genealogies in their villages. David and Samuel the seer established them in their office oftrust. [23]So they and their sons were in charge of the gates of the House of the Lord, that is, the house of the tent, as guards. [24]The gatekeepers were on four sides, east, west, north and south; [25]and their kinsmen who were in their villages were obliged to come in every seven days, from time to time, to be with these; [26]for the four chief gatekeepers, who were Levites, were in charge of the chambers and treasures of the House of God. [27]And they lodged round about the House of God; for upon them lay their responsibility of watching, and they had

charge ofopening it every morning.

The Keepers of the Threshold had great responsibilities. Not only were they charged with protecting the Lord's House from human trespass, but also – as noted - from malignant forces. As such, they were also endowed with strange, mystical powers and it was only through their assistance that certain thresholds could be crossed. To do so without their help could have disastrous consequences. This was directly alluded to in the Book of Zephaniah where people who might attempt to trespass in protected places should consider the danger (Zephaniah 1:9).

[9]On that day I will punish everyone who leaps over the threshold, and those who fill their master's house with violence and fraud.

The Books of Maccabbees have even stronger warnings. These books were written during a particularly perilous time in the history of Israel where extinction was dangerously close and when supernatural defenses were provided by God in various ways. This was the period from which the holiday of Channukah is taken to commemorate the miracle of the oil which burned for eight days.

The Books of Maccabbees were written during the Seleucid domination of the Israelites and is known as part of the Apocrypha which are writings that are not officially sanctioned but are considered of major importance nonetheless.

The next passage was written between 187 B.C. and 175 B.C. during the rule of Seleucus IV, known as Philopater. He was considered the king of Asia but at this period Asia was only measured as the lands which bordered directly onto the eastern Mediterranean.

Seleucus's chancellor was a man named Heliodorus and it was he who devised the idea of ransacking the coffers of the Temple of Jerusalem which was known to hold large amounts of gold and silver. Believing this to be a good idea, Seleucus dispatched Heliodorus to carry out his plan. However, Heliodorus quickly discovered that ransacking the seemingly unprotected Temple of Jerusalem would not be as easy as he'd suspected. He learned first-hand that crossing the threshold of the House of the Lord without consent was a very serious mistake (2 Maccabees 3: 24-26).

[24] Now as he was there present himself with his guard about the treasury, the Lord of spirits, and the Prince of all power, caused a great apparition, so that all that presumed to come in with him were astonished at

the power of God, and fainted and were sore afraid. [25] For there appeared unto them an horse with a terrible rider upon him, and adorned with a very fair covering, and he ran fiercely, and smote at Heliodorus with his forfeet, and it seemed that he that sat upon the horse had complete harness in gold. [26] Moreover, the two other young men appeared before him, notable in strength excellent in beauty, and comely in apparel, who stood by him on either side, and scourged him continually, and gave him many sore stripes.

Quite a reception upon crossing the threshold into the Temple of Jerusalem! Heliodorus eventually escaped but he required several days of recovery from the violent encounter with the supernatural creatures. He returned to the king empty-handed. He did have advice for him, however. And dire advice it was. Heliodorus advised the king that should he ever send another person to burglarize the Temple of Jerusalem it would be best that he sent someone he despised because it was highly likely that this person would be killed.

Keepers of the Threshold have awesome powers at their command and awesome responsibilities. It's a position which requires special dedication.

HEAVENLY BELLS

Bells and ghosts. What could bells, ghosts and the Bible have in common? More than a person might expect. A great deal more.

Throughout the ages people of many cultures have feared ghosts. One type of ghost which was particularly frightening was that of a recently deceased friend, loved one or relative. If a person had been the cause of the death of one of these acquaintances whose ghost suddenly came before him he would be in particularly dire circumstances.

Especially threatening would be the ghost of someone whom one had murdered. When Cain slew his brother Able he found to his great horror that the ghost of his dead sibling would not leave him alone.

The ancient Israelites were among the first to make mourning a stylized ritual. Among the things that the mourner would do would be to don unusual clothing, cover himself with ashes or dirt and tear out his hair as noted in the following passage from Jeremiah 41: 4,5.

[4]On the day after the murder of Gedaliah, before anyone knew of

it, [5]eighty men arrived from Shechem and Shiloh and Samaria, with their beards shaved and their clothes torn, and their bodies gashed, bringing cereal offerings and incense to present at the table of the Lord.

What was the reason for shaving their beards, gashing their bodies and wearing torn clothes? It certainly wasn't going to help the deceased in any way. No. The reason for these various alterations of appearance was actually to fool the SPIRIT of the deceased.

Why fool the deceased? One obvious reason would be to escape its ire if it happened to be angry at you for one thing or another. Another reason to deceive the ghost would be if it had a vindictive nature, no matter the reason. Thus if the spirit couldn't recognise you it couldn't plague you. Yes, the reason for undergoing these various actions was to make a person unrecognizable to the ghost of the deceased.

Another way of warding off the unwanted attentions of a spirit was by ringing bells. It is a method which has been used for thousands of years. One of the earliest descriptions of the use of bells to drive away spirits is in the Book of Exodus.

"And you shall make the robe of the ephod all of blue. It shall have in it an opening for the head, with a woven binding around the opening, like an opening in a garment, that it may not be torn on its skirts you shall make pomegranates of blue and purple and scarlet stuff, around its skirts, with bells of gold between them, a golden bell and a pomegranate, round about on the skirts of the robe.   And it shall be upon Aaron when he ministers, and its sound shall be heard when he goes into the holy place before the Lord, and when he comes out, lest he die.

Lest he die!   This is serious.   It was THAT important that the bells were upon this meticulously designed garment!   He had to be HEARD going in and out.

What is the function of bells on an article of clothing?   Apparently to make noise – why else bells?   The suggestion in this case was for the purpose of making noise to drive away any evil entities in the vicinity especially when entering a religious structure.

This type of activity is reminiscent of the function of the Keepers of the Threshold.   It might've even been likely that they wore similar garments to the one just described above.

Many cultures use sound to drive away ghosts and other spirits. Take for example the office of the Town Crier.   He is a well known character in Colonial America, walking up and down the streets at night, ringing his bell and crowing the time. After calling out the time he would usually end with the announcement: "...and all is well."

It would seem that a person walking around town, ringing a bell and calling out the time would be more a nuisance than a benefit. But he wasn't. In fact, he provided a vital service appreciated by the populous. The noise of the bell was supposed to chase away ghosts, demons and any other evil spirits that might be lurking around the town and not to keep the citizenry awake.

During a period in history when night time was feared for its hidden terrors, people awaited the coming of dawn with anticipation and were relieved to hear the sound of the Crier's ringing and were interested in knowing how many hours were left until the sun would rise.

All types of bells were used to ward off ghosts and evil spirits. Church bells were particularly potent to this effect. During the Middle Ages it was common for church bells to be baptised and specially blessed so that they could be used to dispel ghosts and evil spirits.

In the Catholic Church February the fifth is the Feast Day of Saint Agatha. It is also a night on which witches are said to cavort across the countryside performing evil deeds. In many Catholic cities church bells were rung throughout the night to ward off the witches.

In Rottenburg, Germany Midsummer's Eve was a particularly perilous time of the year and the ringing of church bells from nine at night until dawn was ordered to scare off ghosts and other evil spirits.

April 30th is Walpurgis Night and is known as a major witch's sabbat and it also coincides with the Feast Day of a saint in the calendar of the Catholic Church, Saint Walburga. Once again church bells were used to keep the witches away.

It wasn't long ago when demons and other malevolent spirits were considered the culprits in stirring up inclement weather. Thunderstorms, hailstorms, blizzards – and any other severe weather – were caused by their evil machinations. The furious ringing of church bells was used to quell the rampaging weather. What if it didn't work and the bad weather did not abate? This meant that the people who were suffering from the weather were being justly punished by God – otherwise the church bells would've been successful.

There were certain churches which were famous for their weather-calming bells: St. Adelms at Malmesbury Abbey, St. Germain's in Paris, the bells at St. Pauls in England, and those at Caloto in the Andes of South America.

Sometimes, however, bells were considered to be the playthings of devils. In 1830 there was a mansion in Chester, England which was overwhelmed by the rampant ringing of the bells that were normally used to summon servants. Over a period of eighteen months these bells rang without any apparent cause at random times throughout the day and night.

The owner of the mansion – Mr. Ashwell – called in a special troop of bell-hangers to rewire and remount the bells to fix the problem. Yes – people specialized in performing maintenance on bells used by the wealthy to summon their servants.

One of the series started ringing on its own while one of the technicians was working on them. He leapt from the ladder in terror and ran off screaming that Satan was ringing the bells and that he would have no further part in trying to repair them.

After many more weeks, the uncontrollable bells stopped their disruptive ringing. The cause was never discovered.

Despite this last case, the ringing of bells has more commonly been associated with benevolent acts, be it calming the weather or ridding the land of evil spirits or even helping the dead to find their way to a safe haven.

The Catholic Church of the Middle Ages recognized the use of what was termed a "holy bell." This was a bell that was rung at the forefront of a funeral procession for the purpose of assisting the deceased in his after death journey so that he could escape the path to Purgatory. Although the "holy bell" was not "officially" recognized by the Catholic Church the church did not attempt to prevent its use, however it was left to the deceased's friends or relatives to make arrangements for the bells use.

WARRIORS OF SPIRIT

The Bible is filled with battle upon battle and war after war, covering many centuries of conflict. It shouldn't be surprising that there have been numerous sightings of ghostly saints who are still doing battle against forces of evil.

Two of the better known fighting saints are Saint George and Saint Demetrius. They are formally known in the Catholic Church as "martyr knights." Information about Demetrius' early life is scant, however, the life of Saint George is better documented.

Saint George was born in the mid third century A.D. in the land then known as Cappadocia, which today is part of modern Turkey. Even his name connotes a warrior, originating from a combination of the two words Gerar – holy – and Gyon – battler. It is also highly likely that George at one time was a soldier in the Imperial Roman army.

Saint George is the patron saint of England and the story of his slaying a dragon is well known. George is known for slaying many dragons, not just one. One of the most famous slayings took place in the city of Sylene in Libya. George heard of the dragon that was terrorising this city and offered his services in exchange for the populace being baptised Christians. The mighty saint slew the dragon and the people of Sylene were duly baptised.

Saint George not only fought dragons but he also fought idols set up before heathen gods. In the year 300 George visited a town in Palestine called Lydda. The town was a hotbed of paganism which became immediately clear to the saint upon riding into the town square in which was set up numerous displays of heathen gods.

The martyr knight confronted the pagan idols as the incensed townspeople gathered around. Among the onlookers was the current heathen governor, a man named Dacian. It is reported that Saint George called down a shaft of holy fire from heaven to incinerate the pagan idols before the furious onlookers.

Rather than being frozen with terror, the governor was aroused into a rage and ordered George apprehended. George was quickly arrested and beheaded in short order.

Death did not end his battling for the cause of Christianity. George's ghost continued the fight and was particularly active against the Moslems, especially with the commencement of the Crusades.

Pope Urban II ordered the first Crusade in 1096 after Jerusalem had been captured by the Saracens.   Christian pilgrims to the Holy Land were severely harassed by the Moslems and they were in dire need of protection. The ghost of Saint George came to their aid.

In the book, *History of Antioch,* the ghost of Saint George is described appearing to a priest on the eve of the attack on Jerusalem. He informed the clergyman that if sacred relics were taken into the battle that he would accompany the Christian soldiers and inspire them to great deeds. Saint George's instructions were followed and, according to his promise, his ghost appeared to the crusaders at the walls of Jerusalem at the commencement of the battle.   Greatly inspired by the sight of the saint, the Christian soldiers overwhelmed the Saracens and captured the city of Jerusalem.

Among the Christian leaders present at the battle was Edward III, King of Great Britain.   He witnessed the appearance of the ghost of Saint George and the vitalising affects that this had on the crusaders.   King Edward was so impressed by this that he declared Saint George the patron saint of the military Order of the Garter of which the British king was the founder.

Saint George was not the only spirit to assist the Christians at the walls of Jerusalem that day.   Saint Demetrius also appeared at the walls to aid the crusaders in their quest. Demetrius lived during the fourth century A.D. and, like George, was most likely a soldier in the Imperial Roman army and later became known as a militaristic defender of Christian beliefs. Both he and George were officially proclaimed by the Church as patrons of the crusades.

Another saint who was to provide military inspiration to the Christian cause was Saint Hilary of Poitiers. He flourished during the period of King Clovis's reign which spanned the years 466 to 511 A.D.. Clovis I was the founder of the French monarchy and was greatly indebted to Saint Hilary.

Saint Hilary was elected bishop of Poitiers in 350 A.D.. He was an associate of Gregory the Great and was contemporary of Emperor Constantius who reigned in Rome from 337 to 361. At this time Arianism, which denied the true divinity of Jesus, was a widespread heresy and Hilary was an ardent opponent of this belief. He wrote many theological treatises against Arianism and was made a Doctor of the Church because of his writings.

Clovis was the son of Childeric I who was the ruler of the Salian Franks. After succeeding to leadership of the Salians, Clovis continued to expand his rule and gained control of central Gaul by defeating Syagrius in

486.   His greatest battle was to come against the Arian Visigoths and it was this conflict in which Saint Hilary played a major role.

On the night prior to the anticipated battle, Clovis visited a church that was dedicated to Saint Hilary to pray for guidance. En route to the church Clovis was stopped by a brilliant radiance emitting from near the building. He was startled by the sight and proceeded toward the light which eventually drew him into the tiny secluded building. There, the radiance took the form of the patron saint of the church, namely Hilary.

Clovis was inspired by this and recognized the vision as a divine revelation, predicting a glorious victory over the Arian Visigoths. On the morrow, Clovis administered a decisive defeat to the Visigoths and secured for himself complete dominion of the Frankish Empire.

A warrior who was less known than Clovis had a similar visitation in the mid 600's. His name was Edwin and he lived in the land which was to become known as England. A neighboring chieftan named Ethelfrid was harassing him and while in flight from him, Edwin was captured by Redwald who was ruler of the Angles.

Because of his status, Edwin was locked in a small, dark room rather than being thrown into a cold, dank cell like a commoner. While locked in the room and despairing that he'd never see freedom or his homeland again,

Edwin was visited by the ghost of an unnamed saint. The spirit discoursed with him at length and sympathised with his plight. Then, laying a hand upon Edwin's head, the ghost told him that if he accepted the Christian faith he would escape his prison and would eventually come to rule over all the English lands.

Edwin listened well to the ghostly advice and did accept the Christian religion. As prophesied, he soon made his escape, gathered a powerful army and seized control of England. The authority for Edwin's story is the Venerable Bede, historian for the early history of England.

MORE GHOSTS OF SAINTS AND MARTYRS

The sight of legions of ghosts wandering through a city's streets would be quite shocking. Yet, this has occurred and has received very little notice. Not only has it occurred but it has been documented in one of the most reliable books every written.

The apostle Matthew described the amazing event in one of the gospels in the New Testament (MATT. 27:51-53).

[51]And behold, the curtain of the temple was torn in two, from top to bottom; and the earth shook, and the rocks were split; [52]the tombs were also opened, and many bodies of the saints who had fallen asleep were raised, [53]and coming out of the tombs after his resurrection they went into the holy city and appeared to many.

This of course is a first-hand report of happenings at the moment of the death of Jesus on the cross. Saints and martyrs arose bodily from their graves and wandered through the streets of Jerusalem and nearby surroundings. Unfortunately, Matthew doesn't tell us what happened to the risen saints and martyrs afterwards. It doesn't seem likely that they returned to their graves after an indefinite period of wandering around.

The assumption is that it was the ghosts of the saints and martyrs that appeared to people throughout the city. The use of the word *appeared* is itself provocative in this regard. They *appeared* to people throughout the city. Ghosts and other spectres usually are said to appear.

Unfortunately nothing else is said about this event and it is left as a tantalising phenomenon that corresponded to the moment of the death of Jesus on the cross.

Saint John in the Book of Apocalypse described a similar scene to occur in future times(REV 20: 4-5).

[4]Then I saw the thrones, and seated on them were those to whom judgement was committed. Also I saw the souls of those who had been beheaded for their testimony to Jesus and for the word of God, and who had not worshiped the beast or its image and had not received its mark upon their foreheads or their hands. They came to life, and reigned with Christ a thousand years. [5]The rest of the dead did not come to life until the

thousand years were ended.   This is the first resurrection.

It isn't only the famous that have appeared in one ghostly form or another after death.   A most unusual case is that of a "haunted" floor in a humble home in Belez, Spain.   The astonishing manifestations began in august of 1971 when an Andalusian peasant woman named Maria suddenly noticed a human face in the hearthstone of her kitchen fireplace.

More and more saintly faces appeared day by day until the hearthstone was covered by them. Eventually, a well known parapsychologist was called in to study the situation and a special translucent covering was lain upon the hearthstone to keep the faces from being destroyed.

WEREWOLF IN THE BIBLE

Nebuchadnezzar is a very prominent figure throughout the Old Testament. He is linked very closely to the history of Israel, having brought the Israelites as captives to Babylon around the year 580 B.C. and also having fought a hated enemy of God's people in Tyre.

In many of his battles and victories it is said by word of the prophets that he was acting as God's instrument. Eventually, Nebuchadnezzar himself accepted the rule of Yaweh. But initially, as Paul was the tormentor of early Christians, Nebuchadnezzar was the tormentor of the Israelites (2 KINGS 25:8-11).

[8]In the fifth month, on the seventh day of the month - which was the nineteenth year of King Nebuchadnezzar, King of Babylon - Nebuzaradan, the captain of the bodyguard and servant of the King of Babylon, came to Jerusalem. [9]And he burned the house of the Lord, and the king's house and all the houses of Jerusalem; every great house he burned down. [10]And all the army of the Chaldeans, who were in the captain of the guard, broke

down the walls around Jerusalem. [11]And the rest of the people who were left in the city and the deserters who had deserted to the King of Babylon,together with the rest of the multitude, Nebuzaradan the captain of the guard led into exile.

It was during this period that King Nebuchadnezzar had his many dealings with the great prophet and dream interpreter, Daniel. The King of Babylon was later to attack mighty Egypt itself as was prophesied by Ezekiel who preached to the Israelites during the period of the Babylonian captivity (EZEKIEL 29:19,20).

[19]Therefore thus says the Lord God: Behold I will give the land of Egypt to Nebuchadnezzar king of Babylon; and he shall carry off its wealth and despoil it and plunder it; and it shall be the wages for his army. [20]I have given him the land of Egypt as his recompense for which he laboured, because they worked for me, says the Lord God.

The labour mentioned was the attack on Tyre which was prolonged and ultimately unsuccessful. Why, however, does the Lord begin to treat Nebuchadnezzar as a friend after the king of Babylon had taken His chosen people into captivity?

It's because Nebuchadnezzar suffered through a transformation which left him afterwards quite a different person. The initial stage of this transformation changed Nebuchadnezzar into a creature much like a werewolf. The process is described in detail in DANIEL 4:25, 26.

[25]...that you shall be driven from among men, and your dwelling shall be with the beasts of the field: you shall be made to eat grass like an ox; and you shall be wet with the dew of heaven, and seven times shall this pass over you, till you know that the Most High rules the kingdom of men, and gives it to whom he will. [26]And as it was commanded to leave the stump of the roots of the tree, your kingdom shall be sure for you from the time that you know Heaven rules.

That was what Daniel predicted, and this is what came to pass (DANIEL 4: 28-34).

[28]All of this came upon Nebuchadnezzar. [29]At the end of twelve months he was walking on the roof of the royal palace of Babylon, [30]and the king said, "Is not this great Babylon, which I have built by my mighty

power as a royal residence and for the glory of the majesty?" [31]While the words were still in the king's mouth, there fell a voice from heaven, "Oh, King Nebuchadnezzar, to you it is spoken: The kingdom has departed from you,[32]and you shall be driven from among men, and your dwelling shall be with the beasts of the field; and you shall be made to eat grass like an ox; and seven times shall pass over you, until you have learned that the Most High rules the kingdom of men and gives it to whom he will." [33]Immediately the word was fulfilled upon Nebuchadnezzar. He was driven from among men, and ate grass like an ox, and his body was wet with dew of heaven till his hair grew as long as eagle's feathers, and his nails were like bird's claws. [34]At the end of the days I. Nebuchadnezzar lifted my eyes to heaven, and my reason returned to me, and I blessed the Most High, and praised and honoured him who lives forever...

Which in verses 36 and 27 led to:

[36]At the same time my reason returned to me; and for the glory of my kingdom, my majesty and splendour returned to me, my counsellors and my lords sought me, and I was established in my kingdom, and still more greatness was added to me. [37]Now I, Nebuchadnezzar, praise and extol and

honour the King of heaven; for all his works are right and his ways are just; and those who walk in pride he is able to abase.

It is very interesting to note that in this entire episode concerning Nebuchadnezzar's metamorphosis no mention is made of his being afflicted by any particular illness or being plagued by an evil spirit. He simply changes into some type of beast-like creature which in nature seems very much like a werewolf.

In folklore there are basically two ways that someone can become a werewolf. One way is to be bitten by a werewolf and the other is to have a curse pronounced upon one. It seems that Nebuchadnezzar had been cursed But once he'd accepted the rule and law of God, the Most High, the curse was lifted. This seems the most likely explanation for Nebuchadnezzar's metamorphosis.

CONCLUSION

How are ghosts viewed in general by the church?   While Protestant beliefs diverge from the Catholic beliefs there are certain similarities.

The primary Catholic conception is that ghosts are allowed by God to return to earth for certain periods from Purgatory to do penance for affairs while alive.

But belief in ghosts goes back to the earliest church Fathers. Origen was among the first to write on the topic.   He lived between 185 and 254 and taught in Alexandria and Caesarea.   It was his belief that the spirit of a deceased person proceeded to another plane of existence where it was educated about the things that had transpired in his life and WHY.   In this his beliefs were much like modern day spiritualists.

Origen felt that the soul would progress through various levels of existence, gradually learning the Truth of God's plan.

Saint Augustine had some interesting thoughts on the topic himself. He wrote about the afterlife in a treatise called, *On the Care to be Taken for the Dead.*   Augustine noted that there was a benefit for the deceased to be buried near the tomb of a saint or holy man. According to him, the dreams and apparitions arising from the holy man's tomb would be a benefit to his neighbour.

There were those who believed that God had another reason for sending ghosts to the earth. It was his way of giving evidence of an afterlife to those who were wavering in their faith.

Seeing a ghost could affect a person in a different way. The Puritan divine William Twisse said that he was converted by a ghost. While a schoolboy in the 1590's, Twisse was visited by the ghost of a former chum who revealed to him the agonies of damnation. This was something he certainly wanted to escape.

Taking everything that has been presented in this book into account, instead of being fearful of ghosts or denying they exist, wouldn't it be wiser to seek their aid in the many ways they can offer it? This is especially so since the Bible itself has time and again given credence to the existence of ghosts and their kind by the many warnings given against dealing with them? Why make such warnings if ghosts do not exist?

THE END

XCOXCC